Contents

Acknowledgements

Most of the essays in this volume are expanded versions of papers presented at a conference on *The Professions in Contemporary British Drama*, organised by Daniel Meyer-Dinkgräfe in conjunction with the Centre (now Institute) of English Studies, part of the School of Advanced Study, University of London, on March 6, 1998. The contributions by Mangan, Kurdi and Forsyth were written specially for this collection.

Mária Kurdi has incorporated her longer treatment of John Barrett and Martin McDonagh from her book of essays *Codes and Masks: Aspects of Identity in Contemporary Irish Plays in an Intercultural Context* (Frankfurt am Main, Peter Lang Verlag, 2000). An earlier version of the second part of Daniel Meyer-Dinkgräfe's contribution appeared as 'Writing about Artists: Self-referral in Drama and Society', *Critical Survey* 10: 2 (1998), 52–60.

The Professions in Contemporary Drama

Daniel Meyer-Dinkgräfe

intellect™
Bristol, UK
Portland, OR, USA

First Published in Great Britain in Paperback in 2003 by
Intellect Books, PO Box 862, Bristol BS99 1DE, UK

Published in Paperback in USA in 2003 by
Intellect Ltd, ISBS, 5824 N.E. Hassalo St, Portland, Oregon 97213-3644, USA

Copy Editor:	Peter Young
Typesetting:	*Macstyle Ltd*, Scarborough, N. Yorkshire
Printing:	Antony Rowe Ltd, Eastbourne, UK

A catalogue record for this book is available from the British Library

ISBN 1-84150-047-X

The cover photograph shows Daniel Illsley as Young Beckett in Dic Edwards'
Wittgenstein's Daughter

Contributors

John Bennett is senior lecturer in Drama and Theatre Studies at Liverpool Hope University College. His association with John Godber began in the late seventies when they were both drama students at Bretton Hall College, West Yorkshire, and appeared together in the first production of *Bouncers* at the Edinburgh Festival Fringe in 1977. He was recently commissioned to construct and maintain the John Godber website (www.johngodber.co.uk) and is the author of the entry on Godber in the *Dictionary of Literary Biography* (Buccoli – Clark – Layman, Vol. 233, ed. John Bull). His most recent Godber credit is for the chronology of plays which preface *Godber: Plays One* (Methuen 2001). He is currently completing doctoral research in this area. His other research interests are contemporary popular theatre, playwriting methodology and the marginalisation of northern playwrights.

Peter Buse is Lecturer in English and a member of the European Studies Research Institute at the University of Salford. He is the author of *Drama plus theory: Critical approaches to modern British drama* (Manchester: Manchester UP, 2001) and co-editor of *Ghosts: Deconstruction, Psychoanalysis, History* (Basingstoke: Macmillan, 1999).

Stephen Di Benedetto is currently an Assistant Lecturer in Modern Drama at the Drama Studies Centre, University College Dublin. He received his PhD from Goldsmiths College, University of London in 1999 for his thesis *Playwriting as a Visual Art: A Study of Contemporary English-speaking Dramaturgy Using the Works of Five Playwrights Trained as Fine Artists*. His article 'Concepts in Spatial Dynamics: Robert Wilson's Dramaturgical Mechanics and the Visible on Stage' is published as part of *Space and the Postmodern Stage*, edited by Irene Eynat-Confino and Eva Sormova. He has published numerous book and production reviews in *Theatre Research International*, *New Theatre Quarterly*, *Theatre Journal*, *Irish Theatre Magazine* and *Journal of Dramatic Theory and Criticism*. He is now actively engaged in research on the body in contemporary live art and obscenity in contemporary English dramaturgy.

Dic Edwards' plays have been produced throughout the UK in London, at The Citizens Theatre in Glasgow, Leicester Haymarket, The Sherman Theatre, The Point and Chapter Arts Centre Cardiff and Theatr Clwyd. He has also written two libretti for Broomhill Opera. Several of his plays have been translated into European languages. He is published by Oberon Books, London. Dic Edwards is Lecturer in Creative Writing at Lampeter University

Alison Forsyth has been awarded degrees from the Universities of Surrey, Edinburgh and Stirling. Besides having worked in publishing and administration, she has held lectureships at the Universities of Stirling, Aberystwyth, Tunisia and Bahrain. Dr Forsyth has recently completed a monograph entitled *Gadamer, History and The Classics: Marowitz, Fugard, Berkoff and Harrison Rewrite The Theatre* (New York: Peter Lang, 2000). She has also contributed articles, reviews and papers to a number of scholarly publications and conferences. She is currently working on another book and preparing an edition of dramatic 'rewrites'. Since January 2001, she has been a lecturer in Theatre Studies at the University of Staffordshire.

Mária Kurdi is associate professor in the Department of English Literatures and Cultures at the University of Pécs, Hungary. Her main fields of teaching and research are modern Irish literature and English-speaking drama. Her publications include a book in Hungarian surveying contemporary Irish drama published in Budapest, and a book of essays titled *Codes and Masks: Aspects of Identity in Contemporary Irish Plays in an Intercultural Context*, published by Peter Lang, Frankfurt. Besides these, she has published numerous articles about twentieth-century Irish, American and British authors. She is guest editor of a special issue of the *Hungarian Journal of English and American Studies*, which contains papers about the work of Brian Friel and contemporary Irish literature in general. Since 1998 she has been editor-in-chief of a biennial scholarly series called *Focus: Papers in English Literatures and Cultures*, published by the University of Pécs. She is member of IASIL and a Hungarian consultant for the Zürich James Joyce Foundation.

Michael Mangan is an academic and playwright, who has taught at Universities both in the UK and the US. He is at present writing a book about theatre and the staging of masculinities. His past academic publications include *Doctor Faustus: A Critical Study* (Penguin, 1987), *A Preface to Shakespeare's Tragedies* (Longman, 1991), *A Preface to Shakespeare's Comedies* (Longman, 1996), and *Writers and their Work: Edward Bond* (Northcote House/British Council, 1998). Plays include *The Earth Divided* (1985), *The Fairy Feller's Master-Stroke, Festival* (1988), and *Settling with the Indians* (1991). He currently holds the Chair of Drama in the Department of Theatre, Film and Television Studies of the University of Wales, Aberystwyth.

Daniel Meyer-Dinkgräfe studied English and Philosophy at the Universität Düsseldorf, Germany, trained as a teacher, worked as manager of a computer software company, taught Literature and Philosophy at Maharishi International University, Norway (1989–1991) and German at various schools in London. PhD in 1994 at the Department of Drama, Theatre and Media Arts, Royal Holloway, University of London. Thesis on *Consciousness and the Actor: A Reassessment of Western and Indian Approaches to the Actor's Emotional Involvement from the Perspective of Vedic Psychology*. Since 1994, lecturer, Department of Theatre, Film and Television Studies, University of Wales Aberystwyth; editor of *Who's Who in Contemporary World Theatre* (Routledge, 2000), author of *Approaches to Acting, Past and Present* (Continuum, 2001), and founding editor of the web-based journal *Consciousness, Literature and the Arts* (URL: http://www.aber.ac.uk/tfts/journal).

Contributors

Tim Shields is a Senior Lecturer in English and Applied Studies at the University of Derby. His teaching interests are in the area of drama and film, and the interaction between texts and image-making. He has also worked in the field of creative writing, for theatre and film, and teaches screenwriting on the University's creative writing programme. His current research is into the use of IT for Humanities subjects, and he has recently launched a web-based Shakespeare course.

Introduction

In twentieth and twenty-first century developed societies, some people acquire knowledge, usually through conventional university education, and base their occupation on this knowledge. They are, as Keith Macdonald puts it, members of 'knowledge-based occupations' (1995). They strive to be accepted by society as *professionals*. As professionals, they are in a privileged position in society as far as esteem, acceptance and income are concerned. It is their specialist knowledge that opens their access to the world of the professions, compared with people lacking such knowledge.

Sociology has been discussing the phenomenon of the professions and professionalisation of society quite intensively. Until the late 1960s, Macdonald argues, the professions (and thus by implication its members) were considered to be of a very high moral standard, and on that basis provide a much-needed stability in society. The assumed task of sociology, in this context of definition, was that 'of listing the characteristics of an ideal-typical profession against which actual examples of occupational groups could then be assessed as more or less professional' (1995). In the early 1970s, sociology shifted to study reality rather than ideals, and soon noticed the significance of power in the struggle of members of an occupation to gain the status associated with the professional. Macdonald describes the shift in terms of two questions: the first, '[w]hat part do the professions play in the established order of society?' leads to discussions of the ethical ideal of the professions; the second question, '[h]ow do such occupations manage to persuade society to grant them a privileged position?' (1995) is representative of the power approach and later developments of the *professional project*.

In quite a number of contemporary British plays written and performed over the last 40 years, major characters are members of various professions:

- education (school or university teachers)
- religion (vicars, bishops, priests)
- law (solicitors, barristers, judges)
- media (journalists, publishers)
- medicine (doctors and nurses)
- 'others' (archaeologists).

Each of those occupational groups has been successful in the professional project. In a society defined, with Max Weber, as an arena in which 'classes, status groups and other social entities, such as political parties, compete for economic, social and political rewards' (Macdonald 1995), these occupational groups have achieved a 'monopoly of the market for services based on their expertise, and (…) status in the social order (…)' (1995). They have established the need for a university degree to enter the profession, and have thus gained respectability. Respectability initially enables and then enhances commercial success, because people making use of the professional's services need to trust him or her (their services 'cannot be seen in advance, in the shop window'), and respectability ensures trust. Once the professional has established respectability and trust, economic success will follow, which in turn allows the professional to show more outward signs of respectability, leading again to an increase in trust and economic success, and so on.

Whereas much has been made, in critical literature, of the depiction of working-class characters in contemporary British drama, at least ever since the so-called revolution started with Osborne's *Look Back in Anger*, academia has, on the whole, ignored professionals. *The Professions in Contemporary Drama* fills this extraordinary gap.

Rather than following a set pattern of enquiry established *a priori*, or analysing pre-established criteria over a range of plays with regard to different professions, which would be an approach appropriate to a one-author study, the essays in this collection draw on the different foci of research and subject expertise of their authors, thus leading to a broad range of points of departure, argument and methodology. In the remainder of this introduction, I will place the individual contributions within the context of *professions*, and relate them to the other material presented in this book.

In *Bouncer – Teacher – Doctor: The Gentrification of Godber*, **John Bennett** introduces two issues that are particularly relevant to the topic of the portrayal of the professions in contemporary drama, and which appear, in different shapes, from different perspectives, directly and indirectly, throughout the book: the relation of profession to class, and the dramatist's own position within the framework created by those two parameters. In other words: are the professions typically middle-class phenomena, and, in Godber's specific case, how do we account for the shift of emphasis from working-class characters and subjects to middle-class professionals? Bennett looks at the development of John Godber, considering the change of status in the occupations of the central characters in Godber's plays from 1976 to 2000. He discusses the significance of the nostalgic subject matter of the early plays and the emphasis placed on physicality in, what Godber himself, terms the "sports" plays. He then argues that Godber has developed a third area of interest in his later writing, with a focus on middle-class, professional occupations and a constructed world of class and culture-conflict. Bennett describes these as the "Outsider" plays. He places the texts in the context of Godber's biography and demonstrates a parallel between his changing professional status and that of his characters[1]. The essay includes a useful description of the employment status of the central characters in the thirty-six plays to date.

In dealing with Godber's life, the life of a dramatist, as that of a professional, Bennett's essay also foreshadows the discussion of artists as professionals later on in the book. The professions listed above, i.e., school or university teachers, vicars, bishops, priests, solicitors, barristers, judges, journalists, publishers, doctors and nurses, and archaeologists, appear to have completed their professional project successfully. Their status as members of a profession is beyond doubt. Artists, on the other hand, in their various fields (actors, designers, directors, painters, sculptors, dramatists, poets, novelists, media artists, performance artists, etc.) represent the occupations in the very process of the professional project. To give some examples: increasingly, university degrees are a prerequisite for entering the emerging profession, and actors may find that they have difficulties entering the profession unless they can prove union membership.

While Bennett's essay deals not only with Godber entering the world of the professions, but with a wide range of professions in Godber's plays, **Michael Mangan's** *'Appalling Teachers": Masculine Authority in the Classroom in* Educating Rita *and* Oleanna, focuses on one established profession only, education, and within this on university teachers. Mangan highlights gender issues in two plays whose central characters are university teachers: Willy Russell's *Educating Rita* and David Mamet's *Oleanna*. The contrasts of those two plays are shown on several further levels: juxtaposing British and American cultural contexts in which the plays function, closely related to the differences of time in which the plays were written, and in which the plot is set (1980 and 1992, respectively). Mangan also relates to the subgenres of the plays, comedy and tragedy respectively. Finally, he discusses aspects of what constitutes (breaches of) accepted 'professional' behaviour of the university teachers, in the sense of established norms of good practice within that particular profession. Thus, Mangan's essay deals with aspects of power within the professions, the implications of the gender role in the professions, and with ideal behaviour of the professional.

The next three essays focus on two professions closely related with human welfare: medicine and religion. **Tim Shields** argues that madness as a type of human behaviour *in extremis*, 'in excess', carries with it an inherent theatrical charge. Theatrical aspects of madness may be suggested by such words as mask, persona, utterance, dissembling and concealment, violence and discovery. Those who seek to treat/manipulate/direct/cure such behaviours are likewise put into a protagonistic dramatic role. He seeks to investigate the representative quality of the mind-doctors, as, encased in their White Coats and armed with the authority of medicine, science and the law, they cut a swathe through the discourses of power, gender and Otherness. He draws upon illustrative examples from a selection of 20th century British plays.

Peter Buse compares the representations of the medical profession in two plays from 1969, Joe Orton's *What the Butler Saw*, and Peter Nichols' *The National Health*. In the first play we encounter characters who are defined in the first instance by their sexuality rather than their profession; and in the second play, we cannot help but be struck by the bewildering near-total absence of doctors from the action of a play set in a hospital. Instead of being put out by this initial hurdle (the professions, the subject of this special collection of essays feature incidentally rather than centrally), Buse makes it the object of his inquiry, arguing that there are very good reasons why the actual profession of doctoring takes a sideline in these plays ostensibly about medical health. This argument is twofold: first, that the positioning of doctoring on the margins in these plays is a deliberate intervention into the popular representations of doctors available in the late sixties – in serials like *Dr Kildare* and *Emergency Ward 10* – and that both plays set out to debunk some of the standard clichés of the "caring and curing" doctor of medical melodrama. In this sense, drama is deliberately setting itself against the mass media. Buse proceeds to show what concerns hold together both mass cultural representations and those of the "legitimate" theatre. Both are not so much "about" doctors in the first instance. Doctors may feature or they may be the central characters, but it is the institutions to which they belong (psychiatry in Orton and the NHS in Nichols) which are the main subject, because those institutions, responsible for disciplining and controlling bodies, are what cause anxiety and tension in the audience.

Mária Kurdi expands the political/cultural function of characters who are professionals, an aspect central to the debate of the professions in sociology, and touched upon by Michael Mangan, in considering the ideological function of clerical figures, protagonists, supporting or minor characters, in some post-1970 British and Irish plays. Their mostly tension-laden connection to the existing socio-political order, with its constraints, and/or to the changing concept and historically evolved expectations of the priest's position in the societies of the British Isles, will be the focus of analysis.

David Hare's *Racing Demon* (1990) is discussed as a reflection on the period of Thatcherism, examining the contemporary situation of the Church of England clergy through the confrontation of characters who perceive their job in different ways and shape their attitudes accordingly. In spite of the divergent paths they take, the two protagonists can be seen as characteristic products of the system that polarises people into the unhealthy extremes of feeling too much confidence or too much confusion. Their shared failure is conveyed by their common inability to harmonise the public and the private in their lives.

The priest characters in Brian Friel's *The Freedom of the City* and *Making History* are viewed as mediators of public discourses that interpret and catalyse political processes. Through the corrupt priest figure in Frank McGuinness's *Mary and Lizzie* the essay examines how destructive religion may become if it constitutes a power contentious as well as alienating. The racism of the central priest character in John Barrett's *Borrowed Robes*, which recalls the 1904 pogrom in Limerick, is found rooted in a complexity of ideologically and culturally entrenched personal motifs.

Plays set in contemporary Ireland review the priest's role in the life of a particular community, and through that the impact of faith and religion in more general terms. The authors seem equally intrigued by the question of whether or not the priest still occupies a kind of authority and moral centre. In *Living Quarters* Friel gives a highly unflattering picture of an ineffectual chaplain, the friend of a middle-class family. The priest assumes a positive role in Niall Williams's *A Little Like Paradise*, his function being stressed in spiritual terms. With its postmodern technique, *The Leenane Trilogy* by Martin McDonagh shatters the myth of the West from many angles, depicting a world where brutally committed crimes are followed by the suicide of Father Welsh, due to his depression caused by his failure to reform people.

The final four chapters of the book take up arts-related issues, already an aspect of Bennett's essay in his exploration of the development of dramatist Godber's creative career from working-class to middle-class professional characters. **Stephen Di Benedetto** and **Alison Forsyth** analyse one particular play each, David Storey's *Life*

Introduction

Class, and Tony Harrison's *The Trackers of Oxyrynchus*. **Daniel Meyer-Dinkgräfe** focuses on a range of biographical plays about famous artists, and **Dic Edwards** contributes a chapter based on his own experience as a playwright. Each of those four essays shows different aspects of the artists as an occupational group engaged in the professional project.

The biographical approach forms one element of Di Benedetto's essay when he places Storey's *Life Class* within the context of Storey's biography: Storey trained as an artist at the Slade School of Fine Art in the late 1950s and though he abandoned painting, art and artists still find their place within his fictional worlds.

With *Life Class*, Storey uses the dramatic medium to depict an art school, the medium of establishing respectability. The artist at the plays centre is Allot, who teaches students by espousing an aesthetic philosophy that revolves around the 'invisible event' that takes place when spectators watch the minute and seemingly mundane interactions of life transpire. Throughout the play little dramatic action of any note takes place. Spectators watch scenes where the model poses, the students draw, lewdly joke and are critiqued by Allot, the characters sit down, stand up and make cups of coffee. Storey's control over the playwright's tools of blocking implicit in a play-text allows him to manipulate space using the actor's body on stage as a sculptural form. The interrelation of the actors in the stage environment is meant to articulate ever-changing images for the spectators to experience and contemplate. By looking at those aspects of the production, one can begin to see how three-dimensional stage space and physical bodies create moving visual images that make manifest the professional principles used by artists. *Life Class* is a metatheatrical discourse that contemplates its own form through the discussion of visual art principles and practice. The play has been characterised by critics as plotless, though the plot can be thought of as an 'invisible event' – productions show Allot enacting his professional principles through physical and intellectual interactions with individual students. This 'invisible event' can be thought of as the play in performance, whose content and form are controlled by Storey, unfolding in time as a series of still lives.

In di Benedetto's view, *Life Class* is a play about a professional artist at work, a self-reflexive metatheatrical event and a piece of visual art. Meyer-Dinkgräfe's point of departure is the observation that since the commercial successes of Pam Gems' *Piaf* and Peter Shaffer's *Amadeus*, during the last twenty-two years in Britain the number of biographical plays about famous artists has risen considerably compared with the rest of the 20th century. The essay provides a survey of such plays, looking in turn at their place within the historical context of contemporary British drama, the different ways they deal with their artist characters, and the motivations for dramatists to write about fellow-artists.

Alison Forsyth's interpretation of Tony Harrison's ingenious contrapuntal re-scripting of the extant fragments of Sophocles' Satyr drama, *The Searchers* highlights insights about the role of the professional archaeologist in the 19th century. The historical, time-dependent dimension is also raised by Mangan in his discussion of historical and cultural contexts of *Educating Rita* and *Oleanna*. Forsyth takes this discussion further by showing a late 20th century view on the role of 19th century archaeologists as in the service of a blatant culturally imperialistic project to appropriate the classics. In addition, Forsyth points out, Harrison critiques the very foundations of art, and particularly the Western theatre tradition of which we, the audience, are very much a continuing part. By "rewriting" not only Sophocles' play about the Apollonian domination of the Dionysian spirit of creativity, but also the very archaeological circumstances under which the "fragments" of the play were discovered, Harrison presents us with a disconcerting theatrical accusatory exposition that implicates us, the audience, in the "aesthetic" suppression of "art" at the very moment we are watching the play. Prevented from slipping into a judgmental and moralistic spectatorial repose, we, the audience, are compelled to acknowledge our participatory role in the perpetuation of the commodity aesthetic - albeit in the name of "art".

In the final chapter, Dic Edwards uses his own experience as a working-class playwright to argue specifically that the playwright, too, is a professional. The professional, including the playwright, has a particular responsibility. Looking at, primarily, his play *Wittgenstein's Daughter* (1993), Edwards considers how, e.g. philosophy, which investigates the depths of human purpose, can be subject to the tool of the investigation (i.e. language) with a result that is not necessarily anything to do with the truth. How do we, Edwards asks, get the anti-philosophy of post-modernism? He further queries whether this phenomenon does not extend to other professions, as in the law and journalism so that the professional's responsibility seems to be to the language of his profession rather than to that of society at large. The playwright as much as any uses language.

Not all professions existing in 'real life' and that are represented in contemporary drama are covered in this book, but the individual contributors are addressing, in summary, a good number of specific issues:

- the dramatist's development in the context of the profession;
- the professions as apparently middle-class phenomena;
- the cultural and historical contexts of the plays' contents and circumstances of writing;
- aspects of genre (comedy, tragedy);
- expected professional' behaviour, reflecting good practice;
- aspects of gender;
- the tension between the professional as an individual and a representative of an institution;
- the deliberate marginalisation of professional characters to provide a contrast to their depiction in the mass media;
- an ethical dimension to the professional's work.

The plays discussed in this book may have additional dimensions relating to the professions of their (major) characters to the ones discussed by the contributors. Further dimensions may be revealed by taking more plays into account which have professionals as major characters. Expanding the range to plays from other countries of the world besides the USA, the UK and Ireland, as in this collection, will certainly yield further insights. Plays with members of various professions as major characters need to be further compared with other bodies of plays to establish their relevance in the entire field of contemporary drama ... There is a wide area of unexplored territory here, and this book can only serve as the beginning of a potentially rewarding debate.

Note

1   The dramatist's motivation for writing plays about specific characters is taken up in Meyer-Dinkgräfe's essay in the book.

1 Bouncer–Teacher–Doctor: Gentrification and the Role of the Outsider in the Plays of John Godber

John Bennett

> It became more and more apparent that the world I inhabited – the world, that is, of the industrial West Riding – was an acutely physical one, a world of machines and labour and commerce, and one in which the artist, the man whose work had no apparent use or purpose, was not merely an outsider but a hindrance and a nuisance.
>
> (Storey, 1963)

Not, as you might rightly expect, the words of John Godber but those of the rugby-playing novelist and playwright, David Storey, cited by Godber in his MA thesis (1979). Although the historical decline in heavy industry in the north has moved the employment emphasis from machines to commerce – from hard work to software – for Godber this has not lessened a sense of the artist as outsider; the sentiment expressed by Storey applies equally to Godber. This 'externality' is a key aspect of Godber's writing and one that particularly informs the subject matter of his later plays and their migration from the 'acutely physical' world described by Storey.

In this paper I will outline the representations of work in the plays to date, develop a simple taxonomy suggested by Godber and conclude by interrogating a significant moment of departure from this pattern. I will suggest reasons for this departure and speculate on what this may imply for the subject matter of future plays.

To appreciate the broad significance and personal context of the professions as portrayed in the plays of John Godber it is necessary to spend time outlining Godber's early biography, noting a key event in his childhood, his early working life and considering how these experiences impact on his playwriting. It is crucially important to realise that Godber is a playwright for whom personal experience constitutes *the* key source of theatrical inspiration. He has stated that the five years spent investigating and collating material for his, as yet unfinished, doctoral thesis on the playwright John MacKendrick was 'enough research for one lifetime' (Curtis, 1994).

John Godber was born in 1956 in Upton, West Yorkshire. His mother was a factory worker, his father a miner. Both grandfathers were miners, as were his great grandparents. His parents were keen for him not to continue the family tradition. Godber's father's involvement with the Worker's Education Association convinced him that the key to avoiding the apparent inevitability of working down the pit lay with education.

In 1967, the household was stunned when Godber failed his eleven-plus. The sense of devastation was heightened by the realisation that Godber was one of only three pupils to fail in a class of twenty-five. No comfort could be derived from the assumption that this was a bad class or poorly taught; this was failure on a deeply personal scale (Godber, 1997). It is a moment that still haunts Godber and one that is chronicled in some detail in the 1987 play, *Happy Families* (1992).

The capacity of education to increase social mobility amongst the working classes became, if not common after the 1944 Butler Education Act, then at least possible. It produced a generation of groundbreaking working-class artists, including David Storey. What is distinctive about Godber's relationship to this idea of empowerment through education is that he failed at what was then the first and most critical stage. His parents' chosen escape route collapsed in on him at eleven years of age. Godber now feels that this early academic failure was the beginning of his chronic sense of externality, of being an outsider looking in.

However, Godber went on to do well at secondary modern school and, acceding to his parents renewed hopes for him, rather than his own instincts, trained as a teacher of Drama at Bretton Hall College, West Yorkshire. While at Bretton, Godber's prolific career began in earnest.

Table 1 *The Occupation of the Central Protagonist in the Plays of John Godber*

Play	Year	Central Protagonist(s)
1 *A Clockwork Orange*	1976	Unemployed youth
2 *Bouncers*	1977	Night-club bouncers
3 *Toys of Age*	1979	Unemployed variety artiste
4 *Cramp*	1981	Student
5 *Cry Wolf*	1981	Unemployed youth with special needs
6 *E.P.A.*	1982	Students & Teacher
7 *Happy Jack*	1982	Miner & wife
8 *Young Hearts Run Free*	1983	Students
9 *September in the Rain*	1983	Miner & wife
10 *Up'n'Under*	1984	Painter & Decorator, English Teacher, Butcher, Apprentice Miner, Mechanic, Publican, Health Club Owner
11 *A Christmas Carol*	1984	Clerk and money-lender
12 *Shakers*	1985	Cocktail waitresses
13 *Blood, Sweat & Tears*	1986	Fast wood waitress
14 *Teechers*	1987	School children
15 *Oliver Twist*	1987	Orphan

16	*Salt of the Earth*	1988	Miners and their families
17	*On the Piste*	1990	Radio DJ, Teacher, Record Shop Assistant, Ski Instructor, Car Salesman,
18	*Everyday Heroes*	1990	Professional county cricketer
19	*My Kingdom for a Horse*	1991	History Teacher
20	*Chalkface*	1991	Teachers
21	*Happy Families*	1991	Mining family and student
22	*April in Paris*	1992	Redundant building worker and housewife
23	*The Office Party*	1992	Advertising Executives
24	*Passion Killers*	1994	Journalist, University Lecturer, Business Man
25	*Dracula*	1995	Aristocracy
26	*Lucky Sods*	1995	Club singer turned security guard and video shop worker
27	*Gym and Tonic*	1996	*Builder and Property Developer*
28	*Bloomin' Marvelous*	1997	Author and Lecturer (PhD) Radio Journalist
29	*Weekend Breaks*	1997	Lecturer (PhD) and Screenwriter
30	*It Started with a Kiss*	1997	Student-Teachers and Lecturers
31	*Hooray for Hollywood*	1998	Screenwriter
32	*Perfect Pitch*	1998	Retired headmaster and opera-loving partner
33	*The Weed*	1998	Student
34	*Unleashed*	1998	Business Executives
35	*Thick as a Brick*	1999	Secondary school teachers and parents
36	*Seasons in the Sun*	2000	Refuse collectors*

*This last play's dramatic focus is more aspirational as the central protagonists are students working to earn money to support them while studying at university

This is a chronological list of plays with a description of the work (or lack of it) associated with the central dominant character or characters. Considering the plays prior to 1992, two distinct categories emerge. As Godber explains:

> There's two strands to my work. There's the sporting side – *Cramp, Up'n'Under, Blood, Sweat and Tears, Bouncers* – which are very athletic in their approach. Then there's a sort of lyrical, working-class, almost sort of Stan Barstow, David Storey side – *Happy Jack, September in the Rain, Salt of the Earth.*
>
> (1997)

In 1992, he writes *The Office Party*. This play marks a significant departure for Godber in both form and content. It is the first non sports-based play to demand a single, detailed naturalistic set; the play makes no reference to northern working life; it demands a cast of seven with no multiple-role playing. The characters are all salaried employees in a Leeds-based advertising agency, and although there is the usual hierarchical structure within the office, there is homogeneity of class amongst the characters. The play examines the sexual politics of office life and is played out against the backdrop of the preparations for and the aftermath of the office Christmas party.

The more perceptive critics thought this a radical departure from the concerns of previous work; Beverley Wing, writing in *The Yorkshire Post*, comments: 'Has John Godber, the champion of the working classes, finally turned his back on those closest to his heart?' (1992). Robin Thornber of *The Guardian* is more negative:

> He's tried to aim for the West End by writing one of those brittle, up-market assaults on the amorality of Thatcherite values that we had from writers like David Hare and Caryl Churchill in the eighties. But this isn't Godber's world.
>
> (1992)

That last phrase is particularly telling. This is not 'Godber's world'; neither is the world of the next play – *Passion Killers* (1995). We are now solidly in the territory of the professional classes. The central characters in *Passion Killers* are Tom, a thirty-eight year old journalist, and Andy, a thirty-seven year old businessman. They set out on a golfing holiday to Spain and become entangled, both sexually and otherwise, with other guests at their hotel. Again the play's theme is sexual politics, particularly sexual fidelity within a long-term relationship. The author's note in the programme for the first performance reads:

> In *Passion Killers*, the angle is quite different; (referring to the other two plays in what some critics all Godber's 'Britons Abroad' trilogy, *April in Paris* and *On the Piste*) We take two middle-class British men, and put them jam-smack right in the middle of an alien situation. It is not the foreigners who pose the problems here; it is the other British people abroad.
>
> (1995)

The play marks a gradual geographic drift away from the north of England and a thematic move into comedy of Nineties' class-conscious, sexual manners. Malcolm Rutherford, reviewing the play in *The Financial Times*, made a logical comparison with the expert in this field: '… In terms of output he is becoming almost as prolific as Alan Ayckbourn; and other similarities have developed' (1994). Robin Thornber, ever critical of Godber's work, echoes this observation and questions the success of the transition:

> John Godber moves into Ayckbourn's territory of middle-class infidelity with his latest comedy, but you wouldn't say he's made a complete conquest … Godber's writing always feels more authentic to me when he's evoking his working-class roots.
>
> (1994)

Godber, when asked if *Passion Killers* was a genuine watershed in his career, replied;

> Well, it doesn't have a rugby ball in it. It is a cross fertilisation of my more comic and my more serious work.
>
> (1997)

Or, one might argue, a blending of the sport play and the nostalgia play. How successful this particular hybrid was can be measured by the fact that, despite some positive press from critics such a Michael Billington, the play has never been performed professionally since its first outing in Derby and subsequent tour in 1994/95.

With the arguable exception of *Lucky Sods*, Godber's satirical play about preternaturally fortunate lottery winners, the profession of the central protagonist in the plays has changed fundamentally. As Thornber said, we are now in middle-class territory. *Gym and Tonic* looks at the executive stress felt by an over-worked businessman with an English degree, the TV series *Bloomin' Marvellous* features a successful radio journalist married to a novelist/university lecturer (with a PhD) The hero of *Weekend Breaks* is a screenwriter/university lecturer (with a PhD) *It Started With A Kiss* tells the story of an assorted group of student teachers in the seventies; *Hooray for Hollywood*, a successful playwright turned screenwriter/director. The next play, interestingly a commission from Alan Ayckbourn for his new Scarborough Theatre, is entitled *Perfect Pitch* and set in a scenic spot popular with caravan owners. *Unleashed* considers middle-management let loose in the red-light district of Amsterdam, *Thick as a Brick* argues from a teacher's perspective for a more liberal, arts-based school curriculum, *Seasons in the Sun*, ostensibly concerned with 'bin-men' is an examination of the culture clash between prospective students spending a summer 'on the bins' and their relationship with 'genuine' refuse collectors. It is further distanced from being contemporary social comment by being set in the mid-seventies – again a hybrid of nostalgia and the physicality (i.e. sport) of demanding manual labour.

Why such a change, why depart from the nostalgic content and physicality of form that often led Godber to be described as the third most performed playwright in the country[1] and brought acclaim to a medium-scale touring theatre perched on the north-east coast? I would like to outline some possible personal, pragmatic and aesthetic reasons and to explore the paradoxes this change represents.

On a personal level, it is important not to lose sight of the significant events that occurred in Godber's life in the early and mid-nineties. Firstly, and of the most personal significance, he nearly died. In 1993, a car journey of several hundred miles in a cramped position caused him to develop deep vein thrombosis in his legs which moved to his lungs and threatened his heart. From this point, he starts to get panic attacks. (Godber writes this condition into the male character of his TV sit-com *Bloomin' Marvellous*.) This incident caused Godber to take stock of many things in his life. He married his long-term partner, the playwright and actress Jane Clifford-Thornton; they started a family. These events force him to pause and reflect on the work so far. As he said:

> It used to be plays about big blokes, *Up'n'Under* and *Bouncers*; there are people who think they are the only plays that I have ever written. Now I think it is becoming plays about sensitive blokes, albeit big sensitive blokes.
>
> (1997)

13

It has already been suggested that he writes about the world he knows. He reiterated this position in our last interview: 'I'm always the starting point for the work. And why shouldn't you be, because that's presumably why you are a writer in the first place' (1997). In the twenty-first century, Godber remains a biographical writer, but the circumstances of that biography have changed significantly; 'Godber's world' is now very different. He left teaching in 1984 to become artistic director of the Hull Truck Theatre Company. By the time we get to *The Office Party* he has been at Hull eight years. He has been a professional playwright and director far longer than he was a quasi-rebellious teenager growing up in the shadows of the pit, or rugby-playing, club-going student.

Success at Hull Truck ensures that, albeit on a modest scale, he now routinely deals with advertising people (see *The Office Party*), he's regularly interviewed by journalists (*Bloomin' Marvellous*), his punishing workload means that he suffers with panic attacks and executive stress (*Gym And Tonic*), he's a visiting lecturer (*Weekend Breaks*) and, after *Up'n'Under* the film, a screenwriter (*Hooray For Hollywood*). As he says:

> I go to posh hotels and I know rich people and I've got some money and all the rest of it; should I therefore write about that or should I still write about being the son of a miner?
>
> (1997)

It is not within the scope of this paper to debate the merits, or otherwise, of such a personal approach, but what is significant is that here is a playwright who, having written extensively about his family, their working lives and their leisure-time, then finds his world has undergone fundamental change. Family is still significant, contact with his father and mother vital, but now he is a father himself, in the midst of a successful career and enjoying the most comfortable, although far from lavish, lifestyle he has ever known. The paradox here is that as he grows away from his roots, so the focus of his inspiration swings ever more subjectively inward. The plays become a public dissection of the changed Godber consciousness.

On a pragmatic level, when appointed to Hull Truck, Godber faced an immediate crisis: if the theatre was to survive then box office income had to improve. It was a hard fact of economic life. Certain strategies were closed to him. They could not compete on the large-scale musical front, as that was catered for by the Hull New Theatre, the audience demographic suggested that productions of Ayckbourn would not prove the 'banker' that they do for most provincial theatres; therefore Godber set out on a crusade to win a new audience. The first thing he did was write a play that centred on Rugby League (consciously not Rugby Union, which was his sport of choice at Bretton Hall), the professional game for which Hull was famous. That play was *Up'n'Under* and proved to be a great commercial success. As *The Financial Times* theatre critic wrote, 'The audience came knowing all about rugby and left knowing much about theatre' (Macaulay, 1995). What Godber had discovered was the importance of utilising the 'cultural capital'[2] of his audience. Their expertise and experience of rugby gave them an investment in the play, and Hull Truck began attracting more of a non-traditional theatre audience.

On more than one occasion, Godber has stated that he is now tired of this crusade. His comments to Sheena MacDonald on Radio Four sum up this change of heart:

> Gone are the days, I'm sad to say, where I thought I could single-handedly bring all the ex-miners and ex-steelworkers and ex-shop assistants to the theatre to see my plays, it's a non-starter, that needs massive subsidy now. I've kind of taken the view that I've done all I can do, I've felt like a lone voice in the wilderness for a long time saying to people, look theatre can be great fun, come and have a go, it's great. I feel that I've run out of a little bit of steam. I want to exercise particular aspects of my own psyche, which perhaps isn't as popular as it has been in the past.
>
> (1997)

The paradox here is that a play such as *The Office Party* is still working that profitable seam of cultural capital discovered in *Up'n'Under*. However, rather than a play appealing to the rugby fan, here is a play which appeals to all office workers who have enjoyed/endured an office Christmas party. This allows theatres to try a strategy of niche marketing and can pay high dividends, particularly if canny management stage the production around Christmas time. Local clerical staff may, and often do, choose to celebrate Christmas by coming to see *The Office Party*, complete with party hats, streamers and Christmas cracker humour on-stage and off.

Godber has not abandoned this notion of cultural capital in the more recent plays, just moved it resolutely up-market. One would enjoy the frisson of *Gym and Tonic* more had one personal experience of expensive health farms. The sense of identification for the audience of *It Started with a Kiss* is greater for those university graduates in the audience than it is for those who have not lived through the joys of student life, and more particularly, seventies student life. *Weekend Breaks* makes more sense to those countless thousands who have benefited from their working-class parents' selfless insistence that their children will be better educated than they were. *Perfect Pitch* is aimed squarely at the caravan-owning classes. Godber no longer feels compelled to continue his populist crusade with the same working-class emphasis. The price of buying into the cultural capital of recent Godber plays has increased markedly.

On the artistic level, there is the desire for a new challenge, an understandable reluctance to be pigeonholed as a writer of a particular kind of play. In the early stages of his career, Godber risked being 'typed' as a writer of one style of play, centred on northern working-class nostalgia. The genesis of his latter, physical style was Godber's perceived need to 'raise the bar' of his own theatrical expertise. As late as 1997, he said:

> I find dialogue very, very easy, sometimes too easy, two people talking on a sofa I can do it in an afternoon. When you are actually skiing on stage, or playing rugby, or weight-lifting or doing judo, or playing sixty characters, that's the challenge. What I'm finding now, more and more, is that what I really want to do are the physical plays. And I want to do the physical play because no one else has done them. There is only one Bouncers; there is only one Up'n'Under.
>
> (1997)

These plays have distinct physical theatre quality and an exciting theatrical energy. They owe much to the total theatre concept of Steven Berkoff. *Bouncers* remains the pre-eminent example of this style. By 1997, Godber is feeling the need to pursue a different challenge, as he said in that year:

> There's a kind of game that you play, that you think, well if I do another sports play, people are going to think, Oh! He's done another sports play. 'Oh, he's written another play about holidays – Oh God!' I expect that I will write about experiences other than families and the north and all the rest of it, but having said that, I believe that the best kind of writing is writing which is from the heart.

> (1997)

Godber's heart clearly no longer beats with the desire to mimic the success of formats that built his reputation. He is bravely attempting experiments but, I believe, has yet to find a form to rival the sheer theatricality of *Bouncers*, or a subject written with the same emotional integrity as *Happy Jack*. The paradox here is that, whilst they may break new theatrical ground for Godber – for his audience, his increasingly traditional theatre-going audience, –they appear remarkably similar, almost derivative, of the work of other contemporary comic playwrights.

Finally, Godber's sense of being an outsider is an important factor in his examination of the professions and class in his plays. Godber still feels himself to be on the outside of the middle-class club in general and the theatrical establishment in particular. He labels himself the 'Albert Camus of English theatre':

> I feel like an outsider, I've always felt like an outsider, the plays feel like outsider plays. Since failing my eleven-plus I've felt like somebody who didn't fit in and then being interested in drama in a school where it was a bit sissy to do drama, I didn't fit in. And then at Bretton where I was more akin to the Linford Christie's with a bunch of drama students – I wasn't part of the clique; I was always on the fringes of that, always watching, always on the outside.

> (1997)

It is from this perspective, with deep affection but distanced by education and life-style, that Godber views his family. He also feels that his northern location and his penchant for comedy have distanced his work from metropolitan-based critics. I believe that Godber is now harnessing this detached viewpoint and writing specifically about outsiders – particularly class-outsiders. He is conspicuously juxtaposing characters from differing socio-economic groups as an on-going socio-theatrical experiment. One reading of *Passion Killers* would be to see it as *Bouncers* meets *The Office Party* in Benidorm. *Gym and Tonic, Weekend Breaks, It Started with A Kiss* all are written with the passion of personal experience, but filtered through an outsider's eye – the ex-bricklayer totally out of place in a very upmarket health hydro, or the naïve northern working lad away at college for the first time, surrounded by relaxed, sophisticated students, or the successful academic and playwright trying to come to terms with his perception of the barren life-style and limited horizons of his parents. This is not so much a repetition of Godber as Ayckbourn, but Godber moving into early Mike Leigh, the *Nuts in May* style – a very English drama of character-based, class-conscious embarrassment.

In conclusion, I would suggest that the nineties were a watershed decade for the work of John Godber. He is attempting to create his own style of class-conflict play to complement the success of his biographical and his sports-based work. The most effective example of this would be *Weekend Breaks*, a dark satire on the tension between a professional playwright/lecturer and his aged working-class parents. Although containing similar elements of the new Godber life-style as the other nineties plays, this is a distinctively harder-edged and effectively theatrical piece with the imaginative device of the central character directly addressing the audience as part of a stand-up comedy routine. Godber called it 'a kind of defiant gesture against the luvvies' (1997). Reviews were the most positive for a new Godber play in years, and Radio 4's *Kaleidoscope* devoted half a programme to it, Rony Robinson was particularly exuberant in his praise for the scope of the play, saying: 'The play actually does take on some really important issues like class and who do we love and what really matters in life.' (1997)

If we accept David Storey's initial premise that the artist is a natural outsider distanced from a world of physical work, then Godber's artistic perception must now be doubly distanced – an outsider removed from a cabal of outsiders, distanced from what he perceives as a closed aesthetic community and from his family background in mining. I would suggest that there is now a third broad category of Godber play, to set alongside the overtly physical *Bouncers* and nostalgic *Happy Jack*, and these are the 'Outsider' plays – plays that are naturalistic in form and class-conscious in content – which continue to reflect Godber's own life but are a calculated departure from his established strengths. They may inform the class-debate but, to date, seem to have neither the engaging theatricality of the physical plays or the intimate integrity of the early biographical.

Godber continues to average two plays a year with little sign of slowing down. My third category of play may yet mature into a critically acclaimed and popular format.However, I am conscious that another definition of outsider is 'a contender not expected to win.'[3] One cannot but wonder what the odds are that, in time, Godber may write a play that disrupts his seemingly permanent association with *Bouncers*.[4]

Notes

1. Godber is often described in the press as the third most performed playwright in the country after Shakespeare and Alan Ayckbourn. The source of the information is not attributed.

2. The French sociologist Pierre Bourdieu constructed the term 'cultural capital' to describe the perceived cultural inequalities as opposed to economic capital. Bourdieu, Pierre, 1986, 'The Forms of Capital,' In *Handbook of Theory and Research for the Sociology of Education* ed. J.G. Richardson, 241–58. New York: Greenwood Press. [In French, 1983.]

3. Merriam Webster's Collegiate Dictionary, Tenth Edition 'Main Entry: outsider: Pronunciation: 'aut-'sI-d&r, 'aut-' Function: no Date: 1800

1: a person who does not belong to a particular group

2: chiefly British : a contender not expected to win

    – out·sid·er·ness noun' from www.m-w.com, accessed 2 May 2000.

4. The National Theatre's survey of the 'greatest' plays of the last one hundred years cites *Bouncers* as the play of the year for 1984. Full list can be accessed from www.nt-online.org/home.html.

2 'Appalling Teachers': Masculine Authority in the Classroom in *Educating Rita* and *Oleanna*

Michael Mangan

In this essay I shall be looking at two examples, one English, one American, of ways in which my own profession, that of the university teacher, has been dramatised. During the past thirty years or so, the academic world has provided a regular setting for dramas, from Simon Gray's comically elegiac *Butley* (1971), through to Howard Brenton's scathing satire on intellectual corruption and complicity in *The Genius* (1983). This essay, however, will look at one specific aspect of this topic. Educational and social theorists have long seen the academic profession as a key site for debates on gender issues; and in examining the similarities and differences between Willie Russell's *Educating Rita* (first staged in 1980) and David Mamet's *Oleanna* (first staged in 1992), I shall be concentrating on the ways in which these two dramatists explore issues of gender and cultural authority.

Both *Oleanna* and *Educating Rita* exist in cinematic as well as in theatrical form. *Educating Rita* was made into a very successful film in 1983, directed by Lewis Gilbert and starring Julie Walters and Michael Caine. *Oleanna* was released as a movie in 1994, much less successfully, despite being directed by Mamet himself. Partly because of these screen adaptations, both these plays have had a wide impact on contemporary cultural consciousness – wider at least than most new stage plays can expect – and it may be that it is in their celluloid manifestations that both are best known. It is, however, as theatrical texts that I will be discussing *Educating Rita* and *Oleanna* in the following pages.

Beyond the common professional theme which so clearly unites the two plays, there are a number of structural and thematic similarities between the two plays. On stage, both are two-handers. In both, an older male professor/lecturer[1] (Frank in *Educating Rita*, and John in *Oleanna*) encounters a younger female student (Rita and Carol, respectively). In *Educating Rita*, Rita is identified as a 'mature' student, and we are told at the beginning of the play that her age, at the beginning of the play, is twenty-six (Russell, 1986: 178), while Frank is described as being 'in his early fifties' (Russell, 1986: 169). The ages of the two characters in *Oleanna* is indeterminate, but the mid-career John appears to be about twenty years older than the undergraduate Carol.

Both plays structure this encounter through a sequence of 'tutorial' scenes, in which the primary subject is teaching, but the secondary subject is the power relationships between a man and a woman from different backgrounds. Both narratives are set entirely in the professor's university room, from which claustrophobic and highly-charged environment the stage action never strays. In both plays the outside world is brought into the plot by means of telephone calls; in fact, both plays start with a telephone conversation, and subsequent calls are employed to chart the professors' deteriorating relationships with the world beyond the classroom. Both professors see their personal and professional lives collapse about them during the course of the narratives – although the respective tones in which the two plays stage this collapse differ radically from each other. In fact it is generally true that the similarities which exist between the plays serve also to highlight the significant differences between them, differences which stem from and reflect the times and places which produced them. *Educating Rita* is very much about English society in the seventies and eighties, and *Oleanna* is no less a document of nineties America.

Willy Russell is understandably chary about critics and especially about those critics who insist on finding meanings and influences where he himself intended and felt none, and he has expressed his scepticism specifically about those who 'are bent on finding Samson and Delilah dancing with Pygmalion in Frank's study' (Russell, 1986: ix). Nonetheless, the *Pygmalion* reference is not inappropriate. Shaw's drily ironic tale of sexual and class politics, in which an autocratic professor attempts to take the 'raw material' of a working-class woman and re-make her in his own image, certainly provides a cultural context for *Educating Rita* even if it had no direct influence on Russell's creative process. Like *Pygmalion*, *Educating Rita* stages a world in which it is taken more or less for granted that hegemonic social and cultural authority is most naturally vested in a male figure; and while, like Shaw, Willy Russell subjects this social and cultural authority to a good deal of good-humoured ribbing, he leaves its values fairly intact by the end of the play.

The story of *Educating Rita* is straightforward, almost corny. A synopsis might read: a young working-class woman, intent on getting an education, comes to study English Literature with a rather jaded university professor. Despite difficulties she succeeds in getting an education, and in the process the lives of both the characters are changed. Russell structures the play so that his two characters are presented as embodying two clear-cut sets of social values. On the one hand there is Frank: male, an intellectual, well-off, knowledgeable, middle-class, well-educated and confident in (if rather bored by) his own cultural values. He represents a clearly-defined network of socially validated forms of knowledge and manifestations of achievement, and he has a good stock of cultural capital, which includes not only his books, but his social position and his good taste in art and wine. He watches BBC rather than ITV[2], he owns a house in Formby, a conventionally desirable residential area of Liverpool, and the forms of socialising in which he habitually engages are typically those of the educated middle classes: dinner parties with tasteful wines and intellectual conversation. Frank's identity as a University professor encapsulates all that is conventionally and successfully middle-class – much as he himself might despise the fact.

At the outset of the play Rita is located outside this network of values. Her cultural referents are Eliot Ness rather than T. S. Eliot, Farrah Fawcett-Majors rather than E. M. Forster. To her the word 'Flora' means a brand of margarine; to Frank it is a classical allusion to the Roman goddess of flowers. And so, halfway through the play, when Frank invites her to a dinner party at his house she finds the cultural barrier to be one which she is almost physically unable to overcome:

> RITA: I walked up your drive, an' I saw you all through the window, y' were sippin'
> drinks an' talkin' and laughin'. And I couldn't come in.
> FRANK: Of course you could.
> RITA: I couldn't. I'd brought the wrong sort of wine … you wouldn't take sweet
> sparkling wine would y'?
> FRANK: Does it matter what I do? It wouldn't have mattered if you'd walked in with a
> bottle of Spanish plonk.
> RITA: It was Spanish.
>
> (Russell, 1986: 206–7)

Rita, then, is Frank's opposite. A young working-class woman in an unfulfilling marriage which she sees more and more clearly as being oppressive (and which, like Frank's relationship with his partner, disintegrates throughout the play), she starts from a position of marginalisation. Lacking in much formal education, she is knowledgeable about popular culture but ignorant of the high cultural icons of Frank's universe. Her mind is sharp but undisciplined, and she has a thirst for knowledge which is initially unstructured. The dichotomy is clear. The authoritative and socially empowered male professor is contrasted with Rita: poorly educated, culturally impoverished, socially powerless and a woman. Moreover Frank's professional identity is being used as a touchstone for the author's sense of an authoritative perspective on high culture, and one which the audience is expected to share: the academic as icon of cultural hegemony.

The tone of the play is benevolent, and as a character Rita speaks, in part at least, to those aspirational tendencies in the audience's psyche – that part which recognises the desire for something better, the need to find a fuller meaning in life. At the same time, however, the audience is also encouraged to laugh at, as well as with Rita for her ignorance and her naïveté.

> FRANK: … Have you ever seen Chekhov in the theatre?
> RITA: No. Does he go?
> FRANK: Have you ever been to the theatre?
> RITA: No.
> FRANK: You should go.
>
> (Russell, 1986: 199–200)

Time after time we are placed in the position of knowing better than Rita. We share with the educated Frank a superior perspective from which we are able to find her 'funny, delightful, charming ...' (Russell, 1986: 207). After all 'we', by definition, *do* go to the theatre and are encouraged to lay claim to the kind of cultural knowledge to which Rita aspires.

But while it seems at first sight that Frank represents the interpretative community with which the audience is supposed to align itself, and while this authoritative position appears to be taken for granted, in fact the 'we' is not quite so clear as it seems. Certainly there is not the kind of tripartite cognitive collusion between playwright, character and audience which one might first assume: Willy Russell himself speaks with a voice which is more Rita than Frank. Like Rita, he left his Liverpool secondary modern school with little education and fewer qualifications. More specifically, and perhaps more surprisingly, Russell, like Rita, spent his early twenties working as a hairdresser – 'a job I didn't understand and didn't like. Eventually I even had my own small salon' (Russell, 1986: 164). Like Rita, Russell re-entered education as a mature student: '... as I entered the glass doors of Childwall College I felt as if I'd made it back to the beginning. I could start again. I felt at home' (Russell, 1986: 165).

As the play develops, the initial opposition between Rita and Frank and what they represent begins – as we might expect – to become destabilised. Even in the play's opening scenes these are not portrayed as black-and-white. Frank possesses all the cultural and material advantages, but does not value them. In fact, he has come to despise the professional life which he leads.

> FRANK: Between you, me and these walls, I'm actually an appalling teacher. (After a pause). Most of the time, you see, it doesn't actually matter – appalling teaching is quite in order for most of my appalling students. And the others manage to get by despite me. But you're different. You want a lot and I can't give it.
>
> (Russell, 1986: 179–80)

This twist provides the audience with a way of seeing the relationship between the worlds of Frank and Rita in more complex terms. At the same time as it is invited to adopt a superior, and even a patronising, attitude towards Rita, the audience is offered the opportunity to ironise its own position of superiority. It is presented not only with the opposition between 'cultured' and 'uncultured', but also with that between a jaded, stuffy, and rather old-fashioned world of class-ridden cultural values, and Rita's untutored 'natural' vibrancy, which is rooted in the popular culture which she inhabits. This ironic view of the teacher/pupil is made all the easier for the audience to accept by the fact that Frank (for whom irony is in any case a habitual mode) interprets the relationship in this way too. Consequently, when Rita begins to acquire her education – and so, inevitably, to change – the play begins to raise the question of whether she was actually better off before, with her 'natural' wit and her own working-class culture, and whether Frank's liberal middle-class teaching may have impoverished her rather than enriched her. It is significant that the play is set in – and comes out of – Liverpool: one of the iconic homes of British popular culture in the late twentieth century. But this is the Liverpool of Thatcher's Britain, not of Lennon and McCartney's, and Russell resists any impulse to sentimentalise the Liverpudlian working-class culture which he and Rita have in common:

RITA: … we've got no culture.
FRANK: Of course you have.
RITA: What? You mean like that working-class culture thing?
FRANK: Mm.
RITA: Yeh, I've read about that. I've never seen it, though … I just see everyone pissed, or on the Valium, tryin' to get from one day to the next … 'Cos there's no meaning.

(Russell, 1986: 194)

The events of the play create an epistemological crisis for Rita. The meaning structures of her world are threatened by her new knowledge, and she shows frequent signs of the strain which her cultural realignment is putting her under. However, it is the violent offstage reactions of her husband Denny which most clearly indicate the intensity of this threat: when she will not abandon her studies and return to her role as wife and eventually mother, he throws her out. 'He said it's warped me. He said I'd betrayed him. I suppose I have … But I couldn't betray myself' (Russell, 1986: 209). At one of these moments of crisis, she tells of how, on the verge of abandoning her studies, she went to the pub with her parents and Denny.

RITA: I went into the pub an' they were singing, all of them singing some song they'd learnt from the juke-box. An' I stood in that pub an' thought, just what the frig am I trying to do? Why don't I just pack it in an' stay with them, and join the singin'?
FRANK: And why don't you?
RITA: You think I can, don't you? Just because you pass a pub doorway an' hear the singin' you think we're all OK, that we're all survivin', with the spirit intact. Well, I did join in with the singin', I didn't ask any questions, I just went along with it. But when I looked round me mother had stopped singin' and' she was cryin'. Everyone just said she was pissed an' we should take her home. So we did, an' on the way I asked her why. I said, 'why are you cryin' Mother?' She said, 'Because – because we could sing better songs than those.' Ten minutes later, Denny had her laughing and singing again, pretending she hadn't said it. But she had. And that's why I came back. And that's why I'm staying.

(Russell, 1986: 208)

As we have seen, Frank is also in crisis – a crisis which has begun before the play opens, and which he experiences as a loss of faith in his own professional identity. This leads Frank to question the values on which that identity is built – these being effectively the conventional values of a liberal-humanist approach to culture and education. Although he never seems to lose faith in those values themselves, he does lose faith in his own ability to live up to them. His encounter with Rita brings this crisis to a head. It also forces him to confront the paradox that the relationship between them is predicated upon his professional role as an educator – and thus on his implied capacity to change precisely those things about Rita which he finds most attractive. Frank's crisis is essentially one of authenticity: his own sense that as an intellectual and an educator he is a fraud, and his fear that by initiating Rita into this world of culture he may be making her fraudulent too, and in the process destroying her 'natural' vitality. But while Frank attempts to disavow his position of authority with assertions that he is an 'appalling' teacher, Rita insists in endowing him with all the powers of a priest of high culture. She sees him as its guarantor and guardian, as well as someone with the power to admit newcomers like herself into the noviciate. And Frank is torn between accepting and refusing her projection.

Thus Frank is driven by two opposing impulses: to both reject and accept the role of Pygmalion to Rita's Galatea. And, as in the original myth and in Shaw's early-twentieth-century re-working of it, the gender dimension of their relationship is significant. It is not only as an intellectual but also as a man that Frank possesses cultural power. This is made clear in the way that Frank's professional and personal identities are so closely intertwined in the play. Even his sexual and erotic life cannot be completely disentangled from his professional and institutional existence: his wife (before she left him) had been his muse, and he is now living with an ex-student. Their relationship, it is implied, is an unequal one ('she admires me enormously', he says contemptuously (Russell, 1986: 187)), a hangover from the institutional power which he once had over her. This history of his having a sexual liaison with a student leads to one of the unspoken narrative questions of the play: the question whether Frank and Rita will eventually become lovers. The dynamic between Frank and Rita is always potentially sexual, and all the questions of culture, class and education are underscored by an erotic tension which is central to the play's development.

Erotic relationships are one part of the equation, but the gendering of educational and cultural assumptions is the other. To get a sense of how deeply inscribed the gender roles are within the play, it is only necessary to imagine the different meanings which the play would have had if it had been about the relationship between an older middle-class female academic and a young working-class male student. As it is, the institutional and social power relations which exist between Frank and Rita mean that the dynamic between the older authoritative man and the younger woman is also blatantly patriarchal. It is this patriarchal power which Rita eventually challenges. As Frank becomes more and more certain of the worthlessness of her education, Rita responds

RITA: … What's up Frank, don't y' like me now that the little girl's grown up, now
that y' can no longer bounce me on daddy's knee an' watch me stare back in
wide-eyed wonder at everything he has to say? I'm educated, I've got what you
have an' you don't like it because you'd rather see me as the peasant I once
was; you're like the rest of them – you like to keep your natives thick because
that way they still look charming and delightful.

(Russell, 1986: 228)

This is a very ambiguous moment in the play. Frank has, to a certain extent, been shown to be right in his fears. The more educated Rita becomes, the more she seems to conform, and the more inauthentic she sounds, speaking in forced tones and parroting the pretentious opinions of her new friend Trish. This, it turns out, is a passing phase in her development, but there is no doubt that at this point the audience is being encouraged to agree that Frank has a point. Yet so has Rita: it is precisely her independence, her growing up, that Frank most fears.

Rita's challenge to Frank, and her rejection of his power over her, is couched firstly and importantly in terms of gender (daddy's 'little girl') but also in terms of stereotypes of class and race ('peasant', 'natives'). Ironically, these terms signpost just those discourses of literary criticism which are excluded by Frank's liberal–humanist position. As any feminist colleague of Frank's might have pointed out to him, his brand of literary criticism was quickly becoming dated. Just as *Educating Rita* first appeared on a stage, the professional discipline which forms its subject-matter was undergoing an intense period of self-examination in the UK.

The 'crisis in English studies' of the late seventies and early eighties played on a larger and more theorised scale some of the tensions which are inherent in the relationship between Frank and Rita. For example, Frank's interpretation (which Rita shares) of the relationship between their two cultures is itself a product of a particular kind of thinking about social and cultural structures which is typical of mid-twentieth-century professional literary criticism. It assumes a clear binary divide between high culture and popular culture, bridgeable by the individual – but only at a price. For in order to gain access to that privileged realm of high culture one has to re-make oneself in a significant way. In the case of Rita, Frank fears that the re-making process will be destructive, replacing the attractive naturalness of Rita with a more artificially cultured creation of his own. But a slightly later form of literary criticism than the one which Frank practises would deconstruct this opposition between 'natural' and 'artificial' – and might even suggest that Frank's personal crisis was a crisis both of liberal-humanist values and of the masculine authority which embodied those values. Frank, of course, would have little truck with such an idea. The literary criticism which he practises and teaches is pre-feminist and pre-deconstructionist; it is concerned exclusively with a high-cultural literary canon which is assumed to embody certain kinds of eternal universal values. He outlines his own methodology to Rita

> FRANK: What you have to learn is *criticism* … You must try to remember that criticism is purely objective. It should be approached almost as a science. It must be supported by reference to established literary critique. Criticism is never subjective and should not be confused with partisan interpretation. (My italics)
> (Russell, 1986: 184)

However, even as Frank spoke, his profession was in upheaval, and the apparent certainties of his methodology were being questioned. University teachers in general were becoming less like the independent 'gentleman scholar', and more bureaucratised (Frank and Rita meet in the last few years before Research Assessment Exercises were to drastically alter the status of scholarship in UK universities). At the same time, the vaunted objectivity and quasi-scientific method of the New Critics and their descendants was seen to be untenable, and attention was turned instead to the way in which all forms of literary criticism were implicated in the power relationships which govern their production. Consequently, the relationships between literary studies and wider social issues, particularly those of class and gender – and later, of race as well – were undergoing re-assessment. Academic critics such as Colin McCabe were demanding that literary studies should

> break open the very category of literature – allowing in forms of writing such as science fiction and the thriller. … The first necessity for any course in English literature is to come to terms with that fragmentation of tradition and language which T. S. Eliot did so much both to recognise and oppose, nailing us all to the cross of his own cruel fiction. … It is only when we come to read the broken English of the twentieth century in the tongues of many races that we can then come to terms with the more measured tones of our imperialist ancestors.
>
> (Paulin, 1984: 10–11)

As it turned out, this revolution in English studies was not total. Literary criticism did not, as some had feared it might, become entirely swallowed up by the emerging discipline of Cultural Studies. And if, within the profession itself, those 'teachers and critics who believe that literary culture is no more than elitist bullshit' (Paulin, 1984: 10) turned out to be in a minority after all, nonetheless, things were in the process of changing.

Both characters change, too, though not in the same way. At the end of the play they are both about to move on. Frank is on his way to Australia, where he can rebuild his position and his career. Rita does not know where she is going – except that it is not to Australia with Frank; however she is confident about her own ability to make an informed choice about her life: 'I might go to France. I might go to me mother's. I might even have a baby. I'll make a decision. I'll choose' (Russell, 1986: 231). The erotic tension between the two is resolved by means of the play's final laugh-line: just as it looks as if Rita and Frank are after all about to become lovers, it turns out that Rita's apparent sexual invitation ('I'm gonna take ten years off you …' (Russell, 1986: 228)) is actually an offer to give Frank a haircut: she is not going to become another Julia. The cynical might ask: what is Rita moving on to, and point to the employment statistics for mature students in the Arts subjects, but that is not the point of the play. The point is the personal journey which Rita and Frank both make a journey which is fuelled by Russell's own sense of education as a mode of political power.

It is essential, however, to the dynamic of the play as a whole that Frank represents a generation of teachers and critics who pre-date these changes. The generation which followed him would be less anxious about the possibility that Rita's natural vibrancy would be dimmed by her education, since they would be certain that both nature and culture are socially constructed. They would be less concerned to insist that E. M. Forster is 'literature' whereas Rita Mae Brown is not[3], and more keen to explore the possible connections between the two. They might, too, be more self-aware regarding the gendered character of the institutional and cultural power relationships in which they were both implicated.

The play, like Frank, believes in a liberal-humanist attitude towards both class and gender. It might be argued that as far as gender politics is concerned it is downright conservative. The education of Rita has to some extent redeemed Frank, and in doing so has confirmed his original value-structure. By offering her new meanings, Frank has found meaning in his own life. The play leaves both the liberal assumptions about culture, and the gender structures of the institutions whereby that culture is mediated, more or less where it found them. The assumption that cultural knowledge and authority are essentially the property of the masculine is not changed – and if anything it is reinforced – by the events of the play. In the few years after Educating Rita was first staged, the academic profession (and in particular the profession of literary criticism) became more politicised, more gender-aware, and more critical of the complexity of cultural patterns in a pluralist society than Frank or Rita ever were. But to put the gender politics of Educating Rita in context we need to look at Oleanna.

In Willy Russell's play, issues of gender take second place to those of class and cultural politics. While the cultural authority of the teacher is gendered as masculine, while the teacher/pupil relationship exists in counterpoint to a male/female erotic dynamic, and while the genders of these two main characters could not be reversed without seriously disrupting the meanings of the play, Russell is not primarily intent on analysing gender roles in education. This indeed is the source of the play's conservatism on this front – it exists by default. Except in the most limited way (such as when Rita has her outburst about being daddy's 'little girl') the play leaves assumptions about the implicitly gendered nature of social and intellectual authority intact. In *Oleanna*, however, this gendering of authority, and its implications, is at the heart of the play. *Oleanna* takes this as its the starting point, and turns the teacher/student encounter into a play about gender politics in the university.

If *Educating Rita*'s essential structure is comic, that of *Oleanna* is clearly tragic. Here the teacher's life appears to be about to change for the better. He is on the brink of being granted tenure and things are generally going well for him. His encounter with Carol precipitates a total collapse of all this.

The language of *Oleanna* is a clipped, fragmented language, full of pauses and repetitions. It is a language in which Mamet's stylistic similarities to Harold Pinter are most clearly marked – appropriately enough, since when *Oleanna* was brought to England in 1993 by Stephen Daldry's Royal Court Theatre, it was Pinter who directed it. This English production, like its American predecessor the previous year, generated a great amount of debate about what Mamet has to say about contemporary gender politics. Set, like *Educating Rita*, entirely in a professor's office, this play also appears, in the first Act, to be about theories of education and culture. A desperate female student, on the verge of failing her course, comes to see her professor. She is characterised, in these first moments of the play, as naïve and rather dull.

CAROL: I did what you told me. I did, I did everything that, I read your book, you told me to buy your book and read it. Everything you say I … I do … Ev … everything I'm told.

(Mamet, 1993: 9)

Because the play has only one male character and one female, and because of the way in which the narrative develops, it is easy enough to see these two as representatives of their genders, and as inhabiting typical gender roles. Certainly John, the authoritative, career-minded and overbearing male, dealing with the insecure and (initially) submissive Carol, plays into certain gender typing. But Mamet also plays against type. Like Frank, John is contemptuous of the professional world of academia. But whereas Frank was confronted by his impending failure as a career academic, John has overcome his own early disaffection from school, and has fashioned from that an anti-oppressive theory of pedagogy – one which is currently making his professional reputation.

JOHN: I came late to teaching. And I found it Artificial. The notion of 'I know and you do not'; and I saw an exploitation in the education process. I told you. I hated school, I hated teachers. I hated everyone who was in the position of a 'boss' because I knew – I didn't think, mind you, I knew I was going to fail. Because I was a fuckup. I was just no damned good.

(Mamet, 1993: 22)

John's own ideology is an avowedly anti-oppressive one; he is a radical educator in the tradition of educational theorists of the sixties and seventies such as Ivan Illich and John Holt, whose books *Deschooling Society* and *How Children Fail* criticise traditional education as oppressive and designed to instil failure into children.

JOHN: Look. The tests, you see, which you encounter, in school, in college, in life, were designed, in the most part, for idiots. By idiots. There is no need to fail at them. They are not a test of your worth. They are a test of your ability to retain and spout back misinformation. Of course you fail them. They're nonsense … They're garbage. They're a joke. Look at me, Look at me. The Tenure Committee. The Tenure Committee. Come to judge me. The Bad Tenure Committee.

The 'Test'. Do you see? They put me to the test. Why, they had people voting on me I wouldn't employ to wax my car.

(Mamet, 1993: 23)

Like Rita, Carol begins the play as an outsider, asking for help in entering a world she does not fully understand. But whereas Frank and Rita seem initially to have been mismatched, Carol is the precisely the kind of student John seems to have been best suited to teach. She too, carries around with her the burden of expected failure. 'I walk around', she says, 'From morning 'til night: with this one thought in my head: I'm stupid' (Mamet, 1993: 12). The paradox, however, is that John's radical theories, and his scepticism about the educational system, confuse Carol even more. At one point she bursts out

> CAROL: NO, NO – I DON'T UNDERSTAND. DO YOU SEE??? I DON'T UNDERSTAND
>   …
> JOHN: What?
> CAROL: Any of it. Any of it. I'm smiling in class, I'm smiling the whole time. What are you talking about? What is everyone talking about? I don't understand. I don't know what it means. I don't know what it means to be here … you tell me I'm intelligent, and then you tell me I should not be here, what do you want with me? What does it mean? Who should I listen to … ?
>
> (Mamet, 1993: 36)

Mamet makes much of the contradictions in John's position. On the one hand John's educational theories are about empowerment of the individual student. On the other hand he is confronted by a student who feels anything but empowered – who, on the contrary, is being made to feel stupid for valuing and wanting to succeed within the education system which he despises. 'What can that mean?' he asks about a poorly-written sentence in the student's term paper – insulting and demeaning her in the process. Yet his intentions in his dealings with her are essentially generous. Employing one of the radical tactics characteristic of the 'de-schoolers', he offers to give her an A-grade for the term's work – provided she comes back to see him frequently. He offers to become her mentor, seeing in her precisely the kind of failing and disempowered student with whom he himself identifies.

> JOHN: What's important is that I awake your interest if I can, and that I answer your questions. Let's start over …
> CAROL: But we can't start over.
> JOHN: I say we can. (Pause) I say we can …
> CAROL: There are rules.
> JOHN: Well. We'll break them.
> CAROL: How can we?
> JOHN: We won't tell anybody.
> CAROL: Is that all right?
> JOHN: I say that it's fine.
> CAROL: Why would you do this for me?
> JOHN: I like you. Is that so difficult for you to …
> CAROL: Um.
>
> (Mamet, 1993: 26–7)

Despite the way in which this exchange ends, there is nothing even subliminally erotic about the encounter between John and Carol. In *Educating Rita* Frank was portrayed as being in the throes of the breakdown of his relationship with his ex-student student lover, a situation which allows that play to flirt with the possibility of a sexual liaison between him and Rita. Here, in contrast, the offstage marital relationship which John has at the start of the play appears initially to be comparatively stable. John's status as a family man is established by references to his wife and son, and this is then reinforced by a subplot which involves his negotiations to buy a new house, and which continues throughout his meeting with Carol. A series of phone calls punctuate his pastoral conversation with her, culminating in one which interrupts a moment of confidence which Carol appears to be about to share with him. 'I always … all my life … I have never told anyone this,' she says – but at that moment the telephone rings and we never hear what she had been about to confide in him. In these phone calls John comes across as aggressive, bullying, and self-centred. His attempts to balance the roles of hard-nosed property negotiator and concerned pastoral tutor are clumsy, and in the two discourses between which he continually switches, we see some of the contradictions of his own situation. His confirmation of tenure within the system he despises will enable him to continue the upward social progress, and the benefits which that system has brought him. He is not unaware of this, and is even self-mocking about the contradictions of an educational radicalism which also involves a social conformity: 'The new house. … To go with the tenure. That's right. Nice house, close to the private school. … We were talking about economic betterment' (Mamet, 1993: 33).

The first act of the play is about many kinds of power: the power of the bosses, which John identified in his own educational experiences; the radical educational theories which he espoused in order to fight those power relationships; his own resulting position of professional power within the university system; the extent to which Carol feels demeaned and degraded not only by her inability to comprehend John's academic arguments, but also by his attitude towards her and her aspirations. Even in his attempts to counter one form of educational oppression, John acts oppressively. Yet Mamet does not portray him as a hypocrite or a predator – merely as someone enmeshed in the contradictions of power relationships within a particular social, educational and economic system. There is a delicate balance struck between a liberal audience's potential sympathy for John's original principles, and its more critical awareness of the ways in which these principles are being undermined by John's words and deeds.

It is not until the second act that the conflict between Carol and John turns into confrontation, and the power struggle is refocused as one of gender power. In that gap a month has passed, and Carol has – to John's amazement – brought a series of complaints against him, including that of sexual harassment. This complaint will potentially threaten his tenure, and thus his house-buying and family life.

> I find that I am sexist. That I am elitist. I'm not sure I know what that means, other than it's a derogatory word, meaning 'bad.' That I … That I insist on wasting time in non-prescribed, in self-aggrandising and theatrical diversions from the prescribed text … that these have taken both sexist and pornographic forms … here we find listed … (Pause) Here we find listed … instances '… closeted with a student' … 'Told a rambling, sexually explicit story … moved to embrace said student'
>
> (Mamet, 1993: 47)

The encounter between them, which the audience has witnessed, is re-presented in terms which the audience can recognise as accurate in letter but not in spirit. John's clumsy, and often arrogant, attempts to respond to Carol on a pastoral level, are figured in the complaint as a form of abuse. For a brief period at the start of the second act, as John states his case and mounts his defence, an audience might maintain some of the generally forgiving ambivalence towards John which the first act had established: 'Well, yes, it is possible to see how his paternalistic gestures might be inter-preted as sexual advances, although we can also see that that is not, surely, how they were intended. We saw that his 'move to embrace said student' had been meant as a comforting gesture, not as the sexual overture which the complaint implies. On the other hand, John's radical/liberal stance is more oppressive than he believes, perhaps he does need to be taught a lesson ...' The play, however, does not allow the audience to rest in any such easy position.

The character of Carol is presented in a completely different light from act two onwards. Whereas in the first act she was rarely able to express herself coherently, now she is articulate and aggressive. More precisely, the dramatic and cultural stereotype which she inhabits has undergone a radical shift: from that of The Inadequate Student to that of The Aggressive Feminist. This is explained in the narrative by references to the fact that Carol is now part of an unspecified 'Group' – presumably a Women's Group – who are encouraging her in her complaint against John. Her language is now that of a political correctness which is identified as the voice of that Group, and which becomes more marked as the play continues[4]. She picks John up on the unconscious and casual sexism of his language when he refers to the Tenure Committee as 'Good Men and True':

> Professor, I came here as a favor. At your personal request. Perhaps I should not have done so. But I did. On my behalf, and on my behalf of my group. And you speak of the tenure committee, one of whose members is a woman, as you know. And though you might call it Good Fun, or An Historical Phrase, or An Oversight, or All of the Above, to refer to the committee as Good Men and True, it is a demeaning remark. It is a sexist remark, and to overlook it is to countenance continuation of that method of thought.
>
> (Mamet, 1993: 51)

Mamet has always been recognised as a playwright with an intense interest in language, and in particular with language and power, and the way in which language structures reality. By act three of *Oleanna*, the linguistic stakes have been raised. Firstly, there is no language with which John is able to respond to the charges which Carol is making against him.

CAROL: My charges are not trivial. You see that in the haste, I think, with which they were accepted. A joke you have told, with a sexist tinge. The language you use, a verbal or physical caress, yes, yes, I know, you say that it is meaningless. I understand. I differ from you. To lay a hand on someone's shoulder.

JOHN: It was devoid of sexual content.

31

CAROL: I say it was not. I SAY IT WAS NOT. Don't you begin to see … ? Don't you begin to understand? IT'S NOT FOR YOU TO SAY.

(Mamet, 1993: 70)

This is one of the key moments of the play. In it, Carol asserts her claim, and is backed up by institutional procedures in doing so, to determine what the truth of John's gesture was. It does not matter how John intended his words or deeds; Carol claims the moral right to represent them in her own terms, as an act of abuse. And, as John himself admits, Carol's point of view has something to be said for it. As Peter Lewis, writing in the Guardian soon after the play's UK premiere, put it:

I agree [with Carol]; the meaning of a message isn't totally controlled by its sender – the receiver's interpretation is equally valid. We are not just "ourselves", we cannot escape being also members of a social or ethnic group, perhaps a profession, certainly men or women. In that sense, it wasn't just John browbeating and touching Carol, it was an expression of patriarchal and institutional power.

(Anthony *et al*, 1993: 2)

Lewis, however, was in the minority. Audiences rarely saw much to sympathise with in Carol's relentless pursuit of John's destruction. A more representative response was that of Louise Chunn: '[Carol] is initially insecure and frustrated. But by the end she's a doctrinaire, cold-blooded bitch. A monster of Mamet's making.' (Anthony *et al*, 1993: 2)

The relationship between John and Carol is structured in terms of three acts; the word is meant both in the sense of dramatic structure and of physical action. We might consider the musical equivalent and its corresponding dual meaning: 'movement'. As Mamet has argued,

The study of all theatrical artists should be action. **Movement.** A first test of all elements should be not 'Do I feel comfortable (i.e. **immobile**) when considering it?' but 'Do I feel **impelled**? Do I start to **move**? Does it make me want to **do** something?'

(Mamet, 1993: n.p.)

Each of the play's three acts contains a single significant moment of physical contact between the two protagonists. Because the play is otherwise so language-based, and its physical action so constrained by the office environment in which it is set, these moments of physicality are all the more powerful. In act one there had been the attempt to put his arm round her shoulder. At the end of act two, as he tries to talk her out of continuing with her complaint, John attempts to prevent Carol from walking out of the room:

CAROL: You must excuse me … (*She starts to leave the room*)
JOHN: Sit down, it seems we have a … Wait one moment. Wait one moment … just do me the courtesy to … (*He restrains her from leaving*)
CAROL: LET ME GO
JOHN: I have no desire to hold you. I just want to talk to you …

CAROL: LET ME GO. LET ME GO. WOULD SOMEBODY HELP ME? WOULD
SOMEBODY HELP ME PLEASE?

(Mamet, 1993: 56)

This action, more aggressive than the first, leads to the stakes being raised once again. The charges against John are now being made, not merely to the University authorities, but to the police. It is only at the end of play that John realises that, as a result of this gesture, he is about to be arrested for battery and attempted rape.

Yet in the end it is not this which precipitates the final and genuinely violent confrontation between the two of them, but, once more, language. As John speaks once more into the phone, replying to his wife, Carol tells him, as a parting shot '… and don't call your wife 'baby'.' It is this which finally sends John over the edge:

(CAROL starts to leave the room. JOHN grabs her and begins to beat her)

JOHN   You vicious little bitch. You think you can come in here with your political
        correctness and destroy my life?

(He knocks her to the floor)

        After how I treated you … ? You should be … . Rape you … ? Are you kidding
        me … ?

(He picks up a chair, raises it above his head, and advances on her.)

        I wouldn't touch you with a ten-foot pole. You little cunt …

*(She cowers on the floor below him. Pause. He looks down at her. He lowers the chair. He moves to
his desk, and arranges the papers on it. Pause. He looks over at her)*

        … well …

(Pause. She looks at him)

CAROL: Yes. That's right.

(Mamet, 1993: 79–80)

The action, of course, is devastating. But so is the language – not only in John's use of the explosive word 'cunt', which signals his final collapse into misogyny, but also in the previous line about 'political correctness'. This is a phrase which the play has studiously avoided up to this point. Its use at this point states the obvious, perhaps, but when it is finally articulated, the dichotomy which John has resisted for so long is finally established. It has taken a long time but war has finally been declared – with John as brutal misogynist finally face to face with the powers of political correctness.

Carol's 'Yes, that's right' is a bleak vindication. The oppression, the brutality with which she charged him, has finally emerged. What she sees in his act of violence is the fulfilment of the prophecy which her charges against him constituted.

The play has been seen as a direct comment on Mamet's part on a celebrated academic case in America in the early 1990s, the Clarence Thomas confirmation hearings, which bore certain similarities to the plot of *Oleanna* (Klaus, Gilbert and Field, 1995: 1308). More generally, it is read as Mamet's response to the climate of 'political correctness' in the US academy, and the ensuing paranoia which was engendered among male academics at the time. Mamet's own claim is that the play is not really about sexual politics or political correctness at all.

> I never really saw it as a play about sexual harassment. I think the issue was, to a large extent, a flag of convenience for a play that's structured as a tragedy. Just like the issues of race relations and xenophobia are flags of convenience for *Othello* … [*Oleanna*] is a tragedy about power … The points Carol makes about power and privilege – I believe them all. If I didn't believe them, the play wouldn't work as well. It is a play about two people, and each person's view is correct. Yet they end up destroying each other.
>
> (Mamet, 1995: 52–3)

That the forum in which Mamet expressed this defence of his play was the men's magazine *Playboy* should not, perhaps, impugn it. The context, however, is not irrelevant. Mamet seeks, in a publication which is anything but feminist, to distance himself from the implication that he is simply acting as a spokesperson for the threatened male in the sex wars.

Moreover, Mamet insists that the play's relationship to the Clarence Thomas case is purely coincidental, that indeed he began work on it before the Thomas hearings, and then laid it aside because he was having trouble with the last act (Walker, 1997: 150). Mamet's reading of his own play is not entirely convincing. Certainly the play is 'a tragedy about power', but Mamet oversimplifies it by presenting as far more balanced than it actually is. In *Oleanna* John and Carol do not 'destroy each other' – John is destroyed and Carol is not. It is not just about two correct views; it is about what people *do* with those views.

The problem with the play is that, in presenting Carol in the way he does, Mamet destroys any subtlety which he claims for the play's analysis of power. Ann Karpf, responding to Pinter's UK production, pinpointed the problem.

> Mamet's view is that feminists are deforming personal relationships. But personal relationships have always been inflected by social norms; it's just that most men never noticed it before.
>
> I went to see the play thinking Mamet had dramatised a debate between two viewpoints. What I found was the trouncing of one ideology by another. Mamet is anything but even-handed in his treatment of the characters and issues. He utterly discredits the student who accuses her professor of sexual harassment …
>
> (Anthony *et al*, 1993: 2)

Thus Carol becomes an outright villain, and to that extent the play turns into an anti-feminist polemic. Mamet – in whose work questions of gender and in particular questions about masculinity have always been a central theme – would probably not accept Karpf's general attribution to him of the naïve belief that 'feminists are deforming personal relationships'. Indeed in many of his essays he has dealt quite subtly with gender relationships in a post-feminist world.

In the collection *Some Freaks*, for example, his essay 'Women' is an exploration of gender relationships, in which he acknowledges some of his own confusions about the changes of the past twenty years, and talks of how much men have to learn from women (Mamet, 1989: 22). Thus, the play may not be intended as a backlash statement against feminism. But like John, Mamet is subject to the fact that the message isn't simply determined by the sender. And in this case the message became a decidedly anti-feminist one. It was read (by both men and women) as a *cri de coeur* of the embattled, beleaguered and disempowered male. In several of the performances at the Royal Court, the moment at the end of the play when John strikes Carol was greeted with applause from an audience (or a section of the audience) who interpreted it as an act of heroic resistance to Carol's tyranny (Anthony *et al*, 1993: 2). The critic Geoffrey Wheatcroft reported that at performances of the play in New York, 'there was said to have been fighting between men and women in the aisles', adding disturbingly that 'I don't think any man can yet have watched *Oleanna* without a silent cheer at the denouement when John turns on his tormentor.' Thus, whatever Mamet's intentions, the effect of his play, or perhaps of Pinter's production, was to provoke, in some audiences, an act of symbolic, suppressed or actual violence against women.

The play is, as Mamet says, a tragedy about power – although the way in which the power issues are set up in the first half of the play is more interesting than the way in which they are developed towards the end. More deliberately than *Educating Rita*, *Oleanna* intertwines and explores issues of the academic professionalism and issues of gender. It addresses directly a fear which had become current in American universities in the 1990s concerning the potentially totalitarian effects of political correctness (in act three Carol offers to withdraw charges against John in exchange for his rewriting the course book-list in order to exclude any texts – including his own – of which her Group disapproves). It also portrays a world in which the traditional structures of masculine authority from which John has benefited no longer work. To this extent the profession of the university teacher is being used as an Everyman-figure in an allegory of the late-twentieth-century crisis in masculinity, struggling (and failing) to come to terms with the implications of the feminist intellectual revolutions of the seventies and eighties. These implications do not involve a major shift towards actual material and profession-al equality. The Tenure Committee which is about to judge John contains only one woman, and it seems that the most senior academic positions are still largely a masculine prerogative. But power can operate in many different ways, and the way which most directly affects John is the realisation that he does not even own his own intentions. For the scholar, the academic, used to seeing himself as an independent intellect, in control and in charge of his own thoughts, motives and world-view, this

35

amounts to a particularly intense crisis: Mamet's instinct to set his confrontation of the sexes in the professional world of academia was a good one.

Oleanna is also a tragedy about subjectivity. John starts with one understanding of himself and is then faced with another. The world of academia is a world of competing interpretations, and in this context power is defined by the extent to which one interpretation prevails over another. *Oleanna* shows this in action. John is interpreted as an oppressive misogynist, and so that eventually is what he becomes. In this respect Mamet is quite right to make the reference to *Othello* – another tragic protagonist who is reduced by his antagonist to a stereotype of brutality which he tries so hard to resist. But the gender questions raised by the charges of sexual harassment in *Oleanna* are *not* simply a 'flag of convenience', any more than questions of race and xenophobia were in *Othello*!

Notes

1. In this context, the English title 'lecturer' and the American 'professor' are synonymous. For reasons of euphony with the keyword of this volume as a whole, I shall occasionally use the American sense of the term 'professor' in this essay.

2. UK demographic surveys, nowadays as in the 1980s, use patterns of television viewing as one of their indices of social status. Watching BBC is regarded as a higher-status activity than watching ITV.

3. Rita certainly has the last laugh on this issue. Her real name is actually Susan, and one of the jokes about her cultural ignorance is that she has taken the name 'Rita' because of her wish to identify with Rita Mae Brown, the author of *Rubyfruit Jungle* – a book with which mainstream English audiences in the early eighties were unlikely to be familiar. *Rubyfruit Jungle*, however, is not the steamy pulp romance which its title might suggest, but a witty and subversive novel about growth and empowerment which has since become a minor classic of Lesbian feminist writing. A large part of the novel deals with the way in which a University is unable to cope with Molly, the book's unconventional heroine.

4. Again, *Oleanna* and *Educating Rita* share a narrative structure but differ in tone. Like Carol, Rita's idiolect changes in the course of the play. Like her she has an offstage mentor, Trish, who encourages her in her growth away from the professor. Once again, though, the two plays treat these aspects of the story very differently.

3　Theatricality & Madness: Minding the Mind-doctors

Tim Shields

Bernard Shaw warned that all professions are conspiracies against the laity. Yet notable today is the extent to which we seem eager to turn over so many aspects of our personal life to paid experts. Decisions we might once have thought to manage on our own – the arrangement of our furniture, the layout of our gardens, the choice of our clothes, what we should properly eat and drink, how (and how often) we should 'have' sex – in all these matters we meekly await instruction. There appears to be a desire to offload, to devolve responsibility for our private selves on to suitably 'qualified' others. In terms of our mental wellbeing, witness the proliferation of gurus, counsellors, consultants, spiritual advisers – all equipped with appropriate credentials – ready to intervene in our lives. Every natural shock that flesh and mind are heir to brings forth its complementary handler. It is in this climate of voluntary self-displacement, where people seem to stand back from their lives and view them from a spectator position (trying on this or that 'lifestyle' rather than living a life) that plays dealing with madness find their context. The plays I shall be touching on have much to say about lives being observed reflexively, obsessively. (While from the point of view of those sitting in an audience, of course, these matters have always been a spectator sport.)

First to tease out the sub-title of this paper. The word 'minding' is intended to have three strands to it – firstly, paying attention to, as in: don't pay him any mind; secondly, being bothered by, as in: yes, I do mind … if you don't mind; lastly, the notion of keeping a watchful eye on (possibly) our 'minders'. Also, I use the expression 'mind-doctor', generically, as being more suggestive and ambivalent than any variant of 'psychologist', 'psychiatrist', or 'psychoanalyst'. As I shall be concerned with manifestations of madness in a theatrical context, I shall be speaking in general rather than specialist terms – i.e. referring for the most part to recognisable behaviours on a stage, rather than to scientific or professional categories. Portraits of mind-doctors as protagonists in contemporary plays are not on the whole very flattering. To examine why this might be so, it is first necessary to consider what characteristics – or one might say, what qualities – of their profession are being looked at, and how these are viewed. Mind-doctors control one of the most intimate discourses of power within our culture. They lay claim to the ability and the authority to explain us to ourselves: to tell us *how* and *why* we are as we are. In this respect they seek to define human behaviours, to designate norms and to correct aberration from those norms. Mind-doctors have a say in the construction of identity. They can tell us when our personalities are 'disordered'. They can specify in which direction we are '–verted'. They can unravel our complexes and name them for us. Thus they are in a position to tell us *what* we are – and to that extent, *who* we are. They seem indeed to hold all the keys to the self-knowledge that we spend our lives in search of.

As befits any professional, the mind-doctors are trained to their task; they are initiates. Their training gives them a particular perspective on their material (i.e. the minds of their patients) and a sure means to deal with it (them). The power of the mind-doctors resides in their acknowledged professional status, their ostensive expertise and the supportive infrastructure that sustains it – e.g. asylums, clinics, drugs, electricity. However, the most significant source of their power – and one which, of course, they have in common with other professions – is to be found in their command of a professional language. It is through the use of a specialised, learnt (sometimes learned) vocabulary that the client's problems and needs will be formulated, and then discussed. This language does not allow of any gainsaying, one cannot go behind it because it claims to *account for* everything. It is able to pre-empt criticism, because every attack can be reduced to a symptom. Once a patient is diagnosed as suffering from a certain condition, everything s/he does thereafter offers confirmatory evidence. The process becomes self-validating; an enclosed (and enclosing) system.

But the control of a particular social discourse, as Foucault has made clear, is a source of questionable hegemony, a means of enforcement, of dictating subjectivities. Despite its affiliation to the notion of healing, the mind-doctor's project carries within it then a certain overreaching ambition, what in theatrical terms one might characterise as a species of *hubris*. It purports to travel through dark regions, to uncover hidden secrets, to fight dragons, to engender transformations. Though established respectably within the sphere of the medical, it hovers around the metaphysical. It harks back to magic.

If I have outlined the world of the mind-doctors in a deliberately contentious manner it is in order to point up the issues about their practices that have been variously confronted in the plays I shall discuss. But before doing so, it is worth marking out the ground on which madness and theatricality meet. It may then become clear why playwrights are irresistibly drawn to the activities of the mind-doctors – they are symbiotically entwined with their own.

Madness in theatrical use has a long history, reaching back at least as far as the Trojan Cassandra and her prophecies, shrill but accurate. (The belief that the mad might have access to truths beyond the reach of the sane is shared by many cultures.) But when pondering why the trope of madness has had such a general attraction for playwrights, I would suggest the following.

Madness displays human behaviour in excess, *in extremis*, on the edge – it is all to do with edge and edginess. So it carries within it an electric current, an inherent theatrical charge. It is full of danger and unpredictability. It has a whiff of the anarchic and transgressive, threatening possibilities of subversion. In its technical aspects, madness also shares with theatre notions of masking and dissembling, assumptions of personae. It promises literally unspeakable revelations, introductions to forbidden worlds. By 'unspeakable' I mean things that (a) have no adequate words to encompass them; (b) do not warrant a hearing in polite society. It is appropriate, therefore, that such words should be spoken in a theatre, which is a 'licensed' space, a contained and privileged location. In this location, moreover, private madness inevitably becomes public – thence political – widening out its implications and calling up deep echoes.

Theatricality and madness meet in the arena of performance, where we are required to read (that is assess) things initially *at face value*. Exterior manifestations (behaviours) are our only guide to interior workings (psychologies). The conventionalised image of the patient on the psychiatrist's couch itself constitutes a theatrical model: performer – performance space – audience.

The imbrication of the theatrical with the 'psychiatrical' will be further exemplified by reference to individual plays. In these plays, we shall find the mind-doctor presented as both observer and interpreter of madness, and as mediator in some sense between it and the audience, as well as playing a role as a key protagonist in the 'mad' action, instigating it, seeking to manipulate it.

In reaction to all these elements of the mind-doctoring process, it is perhaps not so surprising that the theatrical response has been a defensive one. That is to say, a critical, often satiric one. Critical of the power and pretensions of the professionals – as might be applied to any profession, but here exacerbated by fear, ignorance and mistrust – and satirical by way of retaliatory attack, particularly directed against the mind-doctors' own self-regard. Not only what they do, but also their motivations are apt to come under scrutiny. In the theatre, the mind-doctors are not allowed to shelter behind their professionalism, claiming a position of scientific detachment. They are pursued on a personal level, and often found wanting. In such cases it is their very claim to status and authority that makes their personal shortcomings more glaring and the hypocrisies underlying their stance more evident to the theatre spectator.

In *What the Butler Saw* (1969) Joe Orton presents the world of the mind-doctors as black farce. With the outrageous events within a private asylum offered as a paradigm of society, those in charge are shown as far madder than those in their charge. In fact, we see no patients at all. Those dragged into the action are unwitting outsiders, visitors to the asylum who find themselves caught up in a sequence of bizarre incidents. The subject matter of the play turns upon varieties of sexuality – which are filtered for the audience through Dr Rance's grotesque misappropriation of psychoanalytic jargon. The only innocent party in the proceedings, Geraldine Barclay is subject to an attempted seduction, random examinations, assaults and injections, has her clothes taken, her hair shaved, and is certified insane – all in short order, despite her frequent assertions that she is a fully qualified shorthand typist from the Friendly Faces Employment Bureau.

Orton's equation of society with a madhouse, with those in authority abusing their power at every opportunity in pursuance of a personal agenda, finds its expression in a baroque exuberance of wordplay. Within this context, the parodied inflections of psychoanalysis seem to fit quite naturally.

RANCE: … Answer me, please ! Were you molested by your father ?
GERALDINE: *(with a scream of horror)* No, no, no !
RANCE: The vehemence of her denials is proof positive of guilt. It's a textbook
     case! A man beyond innocence, a girl aching for experience. The beauty,
     confusion and urgency of their passion driving them on. They embark on
     a reckless love affair. He finds it difficult to reconcile his guilty secret with
     his spiritual convictions. It preys on his mind. Sexual activity ceases. She,
     who basked in his love, feels anxiety at its loss. She seeks advice from her
     priest. The Church, true to her ancient traditions, counsels chastity. The
     result – madness.

(What the Butler Saw, 26 ff)

But while the pleasures of verbal outrage whirl us along, the underlying strain of physical abuse is constantly unsettling. Vocally, the characters remain unabashable, but their bodies are frequently and violently bashed. And in Orton's world, this cannot be dismissed as the common currency of farce. The pervasive atmosphere of aggression bespeaks a world view. It is also noticeable that most of the violence and abuse is meted out by the mind-doctors themselves.

Being a farce, *What the Butler Saw* observes the conventions of the genre. The situations are ludicrous but they build upon one another with perfect logic. After Dr Prentice's first attempt at deception (trying to hide a failed seduction from his wife), events develop their own accelerating momentum. When Dr Rance arrives to inspect the clinic on behalf of 'Her Majesty's Government. Your immediate superiors in madness', he naturally misreads the situation and takes charge of it. Dr Rance's heedless approach to events is made feasible by his absolute confidence in his own authority and his fluency in the language of his profession. As discussed above, it is the total elasticity of the mind-doctor's psychospeak that allows him to accommodate to every circumstance. Dr Rance is never lost for words; Orton builds the comedy and the terror of the character upon this facility. It is also significant that Dr Rance's web of words, in which all the other characters become enmeshed, is woven around no-thing. It is attached to and supported by total misconception. In this case, therefore, the predominant mind-doctor is exercising his immaculate skills in a void.

Two plays of the 1970s, Peter Shaffer's *Equus* and David Edgar's *Mary Barnes*, raise questions about the mind-doctors' efficacy in more sober ways. In both plays it is the protagonistic psychiatrists themselves who anguish over their own practice. Martin Dysart (in *Equus*) does not doubt this ability to 'cure' his young patient, but fears the reductive implications of the process. He sees his task of returning the boy, Alan Strang, to normality as returning him to mediocrity, destroying some sort of inspirational contact the boy has with forces that lie beyond everyday experience, the possibility of 'worship'. The notion that, in removing the 'pain' Dysart will also be removing the 'passion', suggests that Shaffer is something of a romantic, impatient with the confinements of rationality.

The arguments in this play over the mind-doctor's role are largely rehearsed at the personal level – Dysart's self doubts are very much tied up with disappointments and dissatisfactions in his private life. In *Mary Barnes*, the central discussion is between professionals. David Edgar's approach is quasi-documentary, as he offers a thinly fictionalised representation of the book written by Mary Barnes in collaboration with her doctor, Joseph Berke. The whole structure and purpose of mind-doctoring is examined – or rather formally debated – by the characters. Thus the political nature of the psychiatric discourse is looked at within the context of a regime that is striving to be both liberal and practical. The 'anti-psychiatry' movement of the 1960s, as exemplified in the writings of R. D. Laing and David Cooper, strove to radicalise perceptions of what mind-doctoring involved, emphasising the repressive social and political agenda that these writers saw as underlying contemporary therapeutic practice. One of the movement's slogans ran – 'therapy means CHANGE not adjustment'.

The community of doctors and patients shown in *Mary Barnes* is under pressure from within and without. The wider community outside the institution is seen as hostile and those inside are divided on issues both theoretical and practical. Mary Barnes herself, who has come to the place to 'have a breakdown' places immense stress on those around her in the course of her 're-birthing'. As one might expect, the radical nature of this community project draws Edgar's sympathy, and he presents the mind-doctors here as people struggling with real problems, genuinely trying to meet what they see as their patients' needs, and operating on the margins of a profession whose conventional practices (drug regimes and ECT) are seen as antipathetic. The outcome of the narrative is balanced between an optimistic view of recovery (for Mary) and a pessimistic prognosis for those still caught within 'the system'.

With Alan Bennett's *The Madness of George III*, we return to the satirical. Madness is handled within a different dramatic genre, the history play, which allows scope for other types of irony and paradox in relation to the mind-doctor's role. Here, matters of class – or rather, hierarchy and decorum – become significant[1]. King George's doctors are faced with the crucial dilemma of who is actually permitted to lay hands upon the monarch's person. Only when Dr Willis comes on the scene is the balance of power firmly established.

KING: *(Howling)* I am the King of England
WILLIS: No, sir. You are the patient.

(*The Madness of George III, p. 51*)

And to remind the hapless George just what this means, Willis warns him – 'I have you in my eye.'

Bennett derives much of his comedy from historical aftersight, our updated wisdom, making many of the doctors' preoccupations with George's physical symptoms seem absurd. Although his blue urine, in fact a real clue to his condition, is ignored by all but his valets. The later suggestion (explanation?) that the source of George's illness was indeed physical rather than mental just increases the irony of the doctors' pretensions. It even renders dubious the 'success' of Dr Willis, whose mind-doctoring methods seem to have won the day.

As a mind-doctor, Willis confronts the king in a battle of wills (and wits), but when the king attempts to subvert his authority, Willis has recourse to his brawny assistants who have no trouble in subduing the patient physically. Even though he appears to have the king's best interests in view, Willis's use of force is punitive. Bennett comments in the play's introduction, that the audience sympathy for the king – resulting from the pain and humiliation to which they see him subjected (reinforced by Nigel Hawthorne's engaging performance) – rather took him by surprise. His reaction is surely naive, in that when it comes to the *agon* between doctors and patients, it is the latter who are always cast in the role of victim.

Augustine (Big Hysteria) by Anna Furse was first performed in 1991 by the Paines Plough theatre company, of which Furse was then artistic director. By eliding history through poetic licence Furse brings together Professor Charcot and Doctor Freud at the Salpetrière Hospital in Paris, and through this imaginative device is able to show early elements of psychiatry in transition. The two men meet at the bedside of Augustine, a young woman patient whose trauma, it transpires, stems from repeated sexual assaults by her mother's employer/lover.

The key terms of this paper, theatricality and madness, come into intimate conjunction at this point, within this play. As well as being the mind-doctor in charge of Salpetrière, where he studies and annotates cases of female 'hysteria', Charcot is a self-promoting showman. He puts Augustine on display to the public, inducing her, by means of hypnotism and the physical manipulation of her body, to demonstrate her symptoms. As well as being obviously damaged and exploited by this process, Augustine is also seen to be complicit with it. She becomes aware of how she is being used; she 'acts up' to Charcot; she becomes a 'star' – even as she remains a traumatised child.

Charcot's insistence that his patients' hysteria is a matter of 'lying bodies' is countered by Freud's growing awareness that the key to Augustine's illness lies in her mind, and in the dreams and stories that she relates to him. His tentative insights are scarcely developed, however, before Augustine takes her destiny in her own hands, and escapes from the hospital, never to be seen again.

As with Bennett, Furse takes factual historical material and uses it to serve her own (theatrical and critical) agenda. Furse's underlying thesis is that Freud opted out – 'copped out' might be more accurate – from the implications of his deepening insights into the workings of the unconscious and its manner of expression, by reverting back to the idea of patriarchal 'control', the accommodation to sociality, rather than using the power of his method to open up new freedoms. Thus even at its birth, Furse sees the psychoanalytical enterprise as fatally flawed, because it could not deal with, failed to respond to, the radical nature of its own insights. Again, in this play, we have a critique levelled not only against professional limitation, but also personal inadequacy. For all his theoretical daring, Furse would suggest, when it came to practical interventions, that Freud remained a man trapped within his time, his class, his professional ambitions.

As one last, recent example of the exploitation of the dramatic potential of the mind-doctoring world, I shall turn briefly from stage to television production.

Psychos was a drama series, of six fifty-minute episodes, screened by Channel 4 in 1999. This production advertised its 'shocking', 'explosive', 'daring' credentials in its claims on audience attention. But in the event the programme turned out to be more striking as a demonstration of how television, a popular consensual medium, has a tendency to absorb challenging ideas – as a body neutralises invasive germs – into the fabric of its own formatting. Thus the subversive quotient of *Psychos* was gradually diminished by its assimilation into the familiar conventions of a medical 'soap' (cf. *Casualty*, *ER*, etc). The programme soon showed itself more interested in the personal relations between the medical staff than in the traumas of their patients. Indeed the patients' problems became little more than the necessary triggers to fire off the next round of conflict/collaboration (for professional read personal) between the medicos. Thus the explosive potential of madness that we have observed in the 'one-off' stage plays is made safe within the familiar codes of a tv drama series, where we know (expect, demand) the assurance that, whatever the crisis, He and She will be around to spar again next week. Only one slight surprise, offered in the final episode, chimes in with the commentary on the stage plays discussed above. It turns out that the *really* dangerous, blade-wielding character in the hospital, is not one of the assorted 'psychos' who have passed before our eyes over the six weeks, but a troubled young doctor whose own nervous breakdown has been carefully charted from episode one.

So, if we now attempt to draw together some reflections on the contents of these varied productions, a number of shared preoccupations emerge.

It is perhaps unsurprising to find how many examples of madness these plays are focused upon sexuality – because the mysteries of sexuality provide a core complex in the notion of selfhood. Dr Rance with his hands-on approach to the hapless Ms Barclay and his assurance of a best-seller in the theme of double incest; Mary Barnes with her obsessive re-birthing; Augustine with her 'body transformed into a theatre for forgotten scenes' – Furse quotes Helene Cixous' *La Jeune Née* – in each case we find disturbance of the mind related to traumas experienced by, and sometimes relived through, the body.

Also, it will not have escaped notice how many of these plays – and these bodies – involve male mind-doctors practising *(sic)* on female patients. In her Foreword to *Augustine (Big Hysteria)*, Elaine Showalter points out that the play belongs to a long line of dramas based on 'the representation of female hysteria' – she cites *Medea*, *Hedda Gabler*, and *The Crucible*. She also talks about Furse's play as exemplifying the 'psychoanalytic appropriation of women'. Here it is perhaps most clearly suggested how what is ostensibly a medical, i.e. scientific, judgment is in reality a social, i.e. polit-ical one. (As a sociological generalisation in this context, statistics suggest that you are more likely to be designated as mad if you are female, poor or black than if you are male, middle-class or white.)

I hope enough has been said here to describe the general critique that has been levelled against the mind-doctoring profession by some contemporary British dramatists. Anna Furse in her play's introduction summarises the problem in a quotation from Georges Didi-Huberman (L'Invention de l'hystérie), where he says: 'It is the problem of the violence of the gaze in all its scientific pretensions.'

But Furse also says something else in her introduction which leads me on to the last topic I would like to raise in this paper. She says: 'In many ways this play is about language. Who owns it? Who suppresses it? Who converts it? Who re-invents it …?' Well, I hope I have spoken about some of those matters too, in relation to the profession of mind-doctoring. But then Furse adds: 'The language is not only verbal but physical and visual.' Professor Charcot's recording of patient behaviour at La Salpetrièrewas published in a series called *Iconographie*. This notable fact is transposed from history to the use of the contemporary theatrical practitioner.

Showalter speaks of the poses struck by the hysteric patients – their *attitudes passionelles* – as being cultural constructs related to classical French theatre. I would like to suggest that the physical and visual nature of the presentation of madness on stage is the key to its visceral power. In particular I would propose Antonin Artaud's use of the term 'hieroglyph' as defining most appropriately the working of madness on stage. For Artaud, as I read him, the word implies a powerful, composite theatrical image, involving voice, body, sound, light, shape, in a 'held' moment which would print itself indelibly on the sensibilities of the theatre spectator. This notion obviously bears comparison with Bertolt Brecht's use of the term 'Gestus', where a similar concentration of dramatic effect is identified.

Think for a moment of one or two classic embodiments of madness in Western theatre, and I believe you will find that they are encapsulated in a physical image: Agave all unaware clutching the head of her dismembered son; Lear in the storm with the Fool wrapped round his knees; Ophelia floating in wild flowers. So, if you apply the same criterion to modern displays of madness, you will find their power allied to specific images: Mary Barnes appearing naked, covered in shit; King George strapped into a travesty of his throne; Augustine striking the contorted poses of *'la grande hystérie'*. The impact of such scenes upon the sensibilities of the audience is largely due to private concerns we have about the stability of our sense of self. The individual image seen on stage may lodge in our minds as a momentary detail of a performance. Roland Barthes writing about photography in Camera Lucida identifies what he calls the *'punctum'* – that detail of a photographic image that leaps out at us and lodges in our brains. But although that indelible image of madness may be a contained and specific phenomenon, its effect is of fragmentation, dislocation, and deep discomfiture for the spectator.

This is one reason, I would suggest, why playwrights have latched onto the danger-ous world of the mind-doctors. It gives access to material which is inherently dramatic and potentially revelatory. But of equal significance is the fact that playwrights are in competition with the mind-doctors; they are, in a sense, contesting the same ground. For dramatists too lay claim to a linguistic control, They are attempting to hold sway over their audience; to shape thoughts, direct emotions, influence lives and judgements. And so when playwrights choose to put the mind-doctor on stage, within *their* scenario, they are drawing a line around him, containing him within *their* discourse. They are claiming the writer's prerogative – of having the last word. Thus, while critiquing the pretensions of the mind-doctoring profession, they are asserting their own freedoms.

Note

1. Class distinction in madness has long been observed in the theatre, of course. In *King Lear* (IV: vi), the Gentleman talks of Lear's distraction as: 'A sight most pitiful in the meanest wretch,/Past speaking of in a king.' Whilst in another world, Mr Puff in *The Critic* announces: 'Enter Tilburnia stark mad in white satin, and her confidant stark mad in white linen.' The confidant is required to go mad when her mistress goes mad, but she is instructed to 'keep your madness in the background, if you please.'

4   Carry on the Welfare State: Orton, Nichols, and the Medical Profession

Peter Buse

I

1969 was a good year for British theatre and medicine, if not for doctors. In its end of year critics' choice awards, *Plays and Players* included not one, but two plays on a medical theme among the contenders for Best New Play. The eventual winner, romping away with 8 votes, has, like its author, been largely forgotten by the critical and theatrical establishment; the other play, which garnered just two votes, is perhaps not quite as celebrated as its author's life, but is still regularly studied as well as occasionally revived. (Roberts, 1989: 32) To be fair to Peter Nichols' *The National Health*, it did lead a solid after-life: in 1973 it was turned into a film by Columbia Pictures; it has appeared fitfully on school syllabi; and, for readers of Manfred Pfister's (1977) masterful *Theory and Analysis of Drama*, it is an essential secondary source, so often does Pfister draw his illustrations of dramatic technique from it. However, the repute of the play I propose to compare it with, Joe Orton's *What the Butler Saw*, has, it must be acknowledged, waxed steadily, while Nichols' has waned. The gradual reversal of fortune of these two plays from the late 1960s may have more than a little to do with the different perspectives they offer on the medical profession. While they are both critical of the authority and status of doctors, their lines of attack diverge considerably.

The medical practitioners of *What the Butler Saw* ostensibly tend to the illnesses of the mind, whereas those in *The National Health* concentrate on the failings of the body. Orton's farce unfolds in the private clinic of Dr Prentice, a psychiatrist less concerned with the welfare of his patients than the possibilities of adultery his profession affords him. Nichols' play is set in the Sir Stafford Cripps Ward (for long-term invalids) of a large and unnamed NHS teaching hospital in North London. (Richard Stafford Cripps was Chancellor of the Exchequer from 1947–1950 in the Labour government which established the Welfare State. As we will see, the name of the hospital is ironic.) Given the sources of funding for their respective doctors, it seems appropriate that Orton's play debuted in the commercial sector, at the Queen's Theatre on March 5th, while Nichols' piece found its home in the subsidised National Theatre (Old Vic) on October 16th. But I am not suggesting a comparative study of the representations of private and public health care in modern British drama, nor, for that matter, of psychiatrists versus traditional medicine, although that difference obviously informs the alternative directions taken by the two plays. Both plays are rather more problematic than such an approach would allow. In fact, analysing these plays in terms of their treatment of the 'professions' – the subject, after all, of this book – is more than a little hazardous. In the case of *What the Butler Saw*, the profession of the play's doctors is secondary by far to the question of their sexual drives and identities. As for *The National Health*, one cannot help but be struck by the near-total absence of doctors from a play set in a hospital. When they do appear, it is either very briefly, or within a special frame, separated from the main action of the stage. The *profession* itself either recedes from view, or barely becomes visible in the first instance.

Absences and omissions, of course, also signify. If in these modern plays set in clinics or hospitals, doctors, or at least their profession, seem to feature only incidentally, rather than centrally, this too is a phenomenon worth diagnosing. There are very good reasons why the actual profession of doctoring takes a sideline role in plays set in medical establishments. The argument is twofold. First, it is contended that the positioning of doctoring on the margins in these plays is a deliberate strategy, a reaction against the various popular images of doctors in circulation in the late 1960s. That is, both plays (*The National Health* more overtly) set out to debunk some of the standard clichés of the doctor which are found in television melodrama of the period. In this sense, theatre acts as critique of the mass media. However, this opposition of theatre and mass media does not hold for all cases, because the two also share common ground on this matter. The second contention is that neither the mass cultural representations, nor their 'high' culture alternatives, are in fact 'about' doctors in the first instance. Doctors may feature in plays or television serials, they may even be central characters, but the real heroes (which is already the wrong term), are the *institutions* to which they belong. In other words, the real star is not the doctor, but the hospital; the play or programme is 'about' the entire medical apparatus, not any one of its individual functionaries. Profession is eclipsed by institution.

II

Is a dramatic piece 'about' doctors the same as one which 'features' them? Can a play 'feature' a doctor without necessarily being 'about' the profession of medicine? The delicate distinction between 'about' and 'feature' has already been employed without comment in the first section of this essay; it is a distinction which may be fruitfully exploited in understanding the special status of the professions in modern British drama. The distinction was first made by Daniel Meyer-Dinkgräfe in his Call for Papers for a conference held in 1998 at the University of London. In that call, he points out the following: 'Many books and papers have been written *about* the members of the working classes as characters in drama, there is, however, not much *about* teachers, the medical profession, the legal profession … . Yet, many plays have been written which *feature* major characters belonging to those professional areas' (emphases added). The shift in terminology between the first and the second sentences is a subtle and yet a crucial one. If a play is 'about' a topic, a person, a group, we assume that it is the main area of concern in the play – it is the central subject. 'Feature', however, does not imply so much centrality as supplementarity. To 'feature' is to be incidental, even if striking or arresting. A detective serial features a car chase; it is about crime, justice. To return to Meyer-Dinkgräfe's formulation, then, why would a particular play (or the criticism of it) be 'about' the working classes, while another only 'features' members of the professions?

The answer must go to the very heart of the way modern British drama (since 1956) is written about and understood. The story is a very familiar one, so often has it been told. Prior to 1956, the London stage was dictated by narrow middle-class sensibilities which demanded French Windows, fine evening wear, and decanters of the best port on the sideboard. Kenneth Tynan dubbed this sort of play the 'Loamshire' drama and saw in it the death of contemporary English drama:

> If you seek a tombstone, look about you; survey the peculiar nullity of our drama's preva-
> lent *genre*, the Loamshire play. Its setting is a country house in what used to be called
> Loamshire but is now, as a heroic tribute to realism, sometimes called Berkshire. Except
> when someone must sneeze, or be murdered, the sun invariably shines. The inhabitants
> belong to a social class derived partly from romantic novels and partly from the
> playwright's vision of the leisured life he will lead after the play is a success.
>
> (1964: 31)

If such a play featured a working-class character, it would be as a butler, a maid or a gardener – a dramatic facilitating device, but rarely a central part. But all that changed at the Royal Court Theatre and elsewhere over a turbulent decade or so when voices (and accents) never heard before were given full throat. The middle classes were pushed from the limelight and theatre turned its attention to the previously under-represented working-classes. This is the mere skeleton (in caricature) of the tale, but in any account of post-war British theatre, it is difficult to escape some version of this inaugurating narrative. In recent years, the story has come under closer scrutiny – sympathetically by Stephen Lacey (1995, 1999), more critically by Dan Rebellato – but it continues to shape perceptions of all later developments.

There is, then, a short answer to the question, 'Why so much about the working classes and so little about the professions?' The most crucial development in British drama since the war is its effort to include sectors of society other than the class to which professional people, of whatever stripe, belong, that is, the middle class. One might even add that this inclusivity comes at the expense of the hegemonic middle classes. The legacy of this theatrical moment still persists: the middle classes are still often deliberately excluded from the most 'radical' new plays, such as those of Mark Ravenhill (1996, 1999). Ravenhill's focus on an underclass of drug addicts and sexual 'deviants' peripheral to mainstream culture follows a direct line of descent from Jimmy Porter, who was also marginalised and at odds with the establishment. So the middle class was discredited in theatrical terms, at least in the eyes of critics and theatre historians, by the late 1950s and has never really returned to favour. The neglect of the role of the professions can thus be read as a simple byproduct of a much broader phenomenon.

The slightly longer answer would bring us back to 'about' and 'feature'. Not only did the plays of the New Wave feature members of the working class in more significant roles, but they were also, in a fundamental way, *about* the working class as a class. In *British Realist Theatre*, Stephen Lacey has impressively reconstructed an inter-textual framework to demonstrate how plays by Arnold Wesker, for instance, were part and parcel of a much wider intellectual debate about the changing status of the working classes during the so-called Age of Affluence. There was much anxiety on the Left at this time about the erosion of traditional working-class culture and communities by the advances of consumerism and mass culture, and both artists and intellectuals attempted to memorialize what they saw as the qualities of an authentic working-class identity. In many ways, then, Arnold Wesker's *Roots* (1964) is the dramatic equivalent of Richard Hoggart's *The Uses of Literacy* (1958), working out on stage a diagnosis of the current state of a whole class. Plays of the New Wave may have *featured* farm labourers, cooks, cleaners, soldiers, plumbers and joiners, but they were *about* the condition of the entire working class rather than any single vocation.

Can the same be said about the professions in drama? Certainly, Kenneth Tynan's 'Loamshire' had its fair share of professional people; but its plays were not necessarily *about* lawyers, doctors, army officers. A play from the tail-end of this period is a case in point. Terence Rattigan's *The Deep Blue Sea* (1952), a type of lower-middle-class melodrama, features among its characters the foreigner, and former doctor (now disgraced), Mr Miller. His skills as a doctor are instrumental in the suicide plot involving the heroine, Hester Collyer; however, the main focus of the play (fortunately) is not the intricacies of his profession. In other words, the play features a doctor without being about doctoring. The programme from a recent revival at the Royal Exchange in Manchester, tells us what the play is *about*: 'The Deep Blue Sea is a powerful and passionate play which provides an intimate glimpse of one woman's fight between desire and duty in post-war England.' (1997: 1) According to the programme, then, there is nothing particularly class-bound about the play's themes; it touches upon such universal questions as 'desire' and 'duty'. At this point, though, ideology critique pipes up with an objection. So-called 'universal themes' are nothing of the sort. The bourgeoisie, in fact, consistently disguises its very narrow middle-class preoccupations in mythic garb, passing them off as universals. While plays of the New Wave set out to show the specificity of a class experience, the plays they were displacing were intent on concealing the class nature of their content. Roland Barthes, writing at about the same time as Kenneth Tynan's attack on 'Loamshire', was perhaps the most relentless critic of this bourgeois strategy. He put his project thus, in *Mythologies*: 'to account *in detail* for the mystification which transforms petit-bourgeois culture into a universal culture.' (1973: 9)

There are two points to be made here. First, for a play to come clean and admit that it is *about* a specific profession and/or class goes against the very universalizing tendency of bourgeois drama, which attempts to push such elements into the background while foregrounding the inter-subjective drama. Second, it must be acknowledged that the perceived 'under-representation' of the professions (in criticism) is of a different order than the previous under-representation of the working classes. Any discussion of the professions in drama must keep in mind the class interests at stake if it is to answer effectively another important question raised in Meyer-Dinkgräfe's Call for Papers: 'Why has [the representation of professions in British drama] attracted relatively little academic analysis?'

III

There has, in fact, been some quite substantial academic analysis of the way the medical profession is represented, but it has not tended to focus on theatre. Instead, it is within the disciplines of Media and Communication Studies that the key explorations have been made. Consequently, much has been written about the way doctors and nurses are portrayed by the media and particularly on television (Karpf, 1988; Turow, 1989). This is only to be expected, since the genre most responsible for dissemination of popular ideas about the medical profession is the medical melodrama. Very rarely do we encounter stage plays set directly in a medical working environment, but countless television programmes show us nothing but the daily activities of hospitals – most commonly emergency wards. This context provides the ready-made materials of melodrama: the struggle between life and death, the heroic acts of doctors and medicine against the villainy of disease and human violence. It may be precisely the rather stark and crude formulae of melodrama which discourage many traditional drama critics from interrogating the varying representations of the medical profession. Nonetheless, it is to *ER*, *Casualty*, *Chicago Hope*, *Cardiac Arrest*, *St. Elsewhere*, and *Peak Practice* that we must turn if we want to see doctors *as* doctors rather than as members of the bourgeoisie first and doctors only incidentally. Furthermore, medical melodrama inevitably informs the way doctors are represented on stage, since there is always a cross-fertilisation between popular representations and their more highbrow cousins. *What the Butler Saw* and *The National Health* are no exception to this rule and they actively engage with the meanings in circulation about medicine in their time.

Julia Hallam's significant work on this subject reveals that the medical serial as we know it now in the form of *ER* and *Casualty* has mutated substantially since Orton and Nichols were writing their plays. In the typical medical melodrama of the 1990s

> The hospital is no longer imagined as a place of peace, sanctity and refuge where care and control of the body can be safely rescinded to others and problems will be solved, but as a tense, nervous environment constantly disrupted by uncontrollable events. Crises are precipitated not only by a constant influx of sick and injured people but by a lack of resources, attacks from distraught users, and strained emotional relationships between the staff[2].
>
> (Hallam, 1997: 14)

This picture of barely restrained chaos is far removed from the average British medical serial of 1969, when an optimism about the powers of biomedicine still prevailed and where the doctor still commanded respect as a healer.

The first continuing medical melodrama on British television, *Emergency Ward 10*, ran from 1962 to 1972 on ITV, covering the same period as American serials such as

Marcus Welby and *Ben Casey*. These serials emerged at a time when medical technology was making impressive advances (antibiotics, heart transplants) and the National Health Service was still widely regarded as a proud pillar of the Welfare State. The general confidence in the medical profession was embodied in the doctor figure, the uncompromised hero of the medical melodrama:

> Traditionally in medical melodrama, the doctor figure can be seen as a personification of moral and ethical values, his relationship with the patient the locus around which the disease or illness embodied in the patient is cured through a combination of technical skill and psychic restoration. The split between body and mind, now seen as a problem of contemporary medicine, is held together in the figure of the handsome young doctor who not only cures but cares.

(1997: 8)

Hallam adds that 'the saintly demeanour, high moral character, and good looks of the archetypal television doctor added weight to analogies in popular fiction of doctors as god-like, larger-than-life characters with magical powers to create health and well-being.' (1997: 3) In other words, through the medical melodrama, a powerful fantasy of the omnipotent and altruistic doctor was well established in the popular imagination by the late 1960s. At this historical juncture, then, the medical profession provided the site for an elaborate wish-fulfillment: doctors can not only be trusted to put right the physical ailments of individuals, but can be invested with the potential to heal the fissures in society. The social function of such a figure is explored at length by Hallam, Turow and Karpf. More important for present purposes is the way this melodramatic hero, clearly so ripe for demystification, measures up to his counterparts and contemporaries in *The National Health* and *What the Butler Saw*.

IV

The National Health and *What the Butler Saw* are both highly sceptical of the idealisation of the doctor found in television serials and both set out to dent this squeaky clean image of the heroic and ethical doctor. Nichols does this by juxtaposing the myth of the benevolent doctor with the grim realities of everyday life in a hospital ward for the long term ill. Orton reinvigorates the farcical mode by taking the power-knowledge network invested in the psychiatric discipline to its logical and hysterical extremes. His doctors are as unethical as you could wish for, cynically exploiting their professional privileges for the purposes of seduction.

The National Health presents its audience with three separate theatrical levels within the setting of one hospital ward. The main action, or rather lack of action, involves the daily routines of six patients suffering from ailments ranging from stomach ulcers to a coronary. As the play proceeds, four of them die and some are replaced by new patients – this is as far as it goes in terms of plot development. Instead of sustained action on this first theatrical level, we are presented with the mundanity and boredom of the patients' lives in the hospital. Their days are punctuated by trips to the toilet or use of the bedpan, the humiliation of being washed by nurses, reflections on ailments and on forced tapioca and semolina diets, and therapeutic basket-weaving. Because this is a 'State of the Nation' play performed in the National Theatre, there are also plentiful debates amongst the patients about the relative merits and failings of the NHS and the Welfare State. The patient Ash takes the lead in these discussions, and the conclusion seems to be that, for better or for worse, the National Health is a TOTAL system, infiltrating its citizens' lives along a continuum:

> LOACH: Babies over there ... cemetery behind the car park ... I don't know.
> ASH: There's your National Health, friend. Look after you from the cradle to the grave.
> LOACH: Marvellous, isn't it? Ah! Sod it!
>
> (Nichols, 1970: 164–5)

The dominant tone in these sections of the play is gallows humour about physical decay combined with thinly disguised staged debates about the Welfare State. We are given to understand that the NHS hospital is more of a way-station than a place for the miracles of medicine. Most notably, nurses are shown to be the main workers within this system, dealing with the day-to-day running of the ward and most of the treatment of the patients, while doctors only breeze through the ward on a single occasion. According to Hallam, little has changed, some thirty years on, in the division of labour in hospitals:

> The health service in Britain provides a particularly acute example of how twenty years of enactment of sexual discrimination policies have had limited success in shifting entrenched patterns of gendered identity in what is in essence a female dominated working environment. Women constitute more than 75% of the NHS workforce, predominantly occupying lower paid servicing roles in disproportion to their numbers overall.
>
> (1997: 5)

It should come as no surprise that Nichols produces this sort of critique at such an early stage, given his close attention to the treatment of the terminally ill in *A Day in the Death of Joe Egg* (1967).

If doctors play little part in the daily routine of the ward, one might at least expect them to appear in moments of real emergency, but this is not the case either. However, situations of extremity – deaths and preparations for surgery – do initiate the second theatrical level at work in the play. This level is orchestrated by Barnet, an orderly, who functions as an epic figure, addressing the audience directly and engaging them with a kind of music hall banter. He appears at the point when the nurses have to deal with the incontinence of the disturbed patient Rees (tellingly a former doctor himself); again when Rees dies, Barnet takes the audience through the unpleasant dealings with the corpse in graphic detail; and he takes similar pleasure in relating the indignities of the preparations for surgery undergone by Ash. These passages all serve to undermine the usual solemnity attached to the powers of medical science, and reinforce the *absence* of doctors from these seemingly crucial hospital activities.

Where the doctors DO appear, in the third theatrical level of the play, Barnet once again serves as the epic mediating device. One of the ways the patients pass their time is in watching a medical television serial featuring the same doctors and nurses who minister to them in the Sir Stafford Cripps ward. This is where the play's sub-title (*Nurse Norton's Affair*) comes in. Here at last, in caricature, we find the life-giving doctors, dedicated to the welfare of their patients and the greater good of humanity, whilst still sparing time for romances with nurses. Barnet narrates from the perspective of Staff Nurse Norton, who holds a flame for one of the doctors, and Nichols holds nothing back in pastiching the style of pulp medical fiction:

BARNET: In the submarine strangeness of the night ward, young Doctor Neil Boyd's
fingers had fleetingly touched hers. And his usually stern features had
crumpled into a yearning smile. Their eyes had met and ricocheted away.
STAFF: This won't do.
BARNET: She chastised herself.

(26)

Nurse Norton holds Dr Boyd in the same esteem as the medical serials of the 1960s held the profession, and this esteem is shown to be justified in the encounters between Dr Boyd and his father, also a doctor. As in those television serials of the 1960s, the ethical dimensions of the doctor-patient relationship concern them to an improbable degree:

NEIL: If it's about the informality of my ward-rounds, you can save your breath to
cool your porridge. I believe I am the patients' servant, not the other way
round. I'm not going to have a lot of ceremony –
BOYD: Now, now, dinna fash yesel. It's noo that. We agree to differ on the question of
how to treat our fellows.
NEIL: Aye. You, the firm believer, seem to regard the weak and infirm as inferiors. I,
the sceptic, behave to them as my equals.

(34)

The medical and emotional dramas of this third theatrical level of *The National Health* resolve themselves in true melodramatic fashion, but in doing so simply show how far removed they are from the 'true' everyday realities of the hospital in the Welfare State. It seems, then, that doctors can only be represented in 'serious' drama at one remove (framed in this case by parody and juxtaposition) because they are overdetermined by popular representations – representations which Nichols sees it as his task to debunk. In other words, he does not attempt an alternative representation of a weak, all too human doctor, who fails to live up to the requirements of the profession, but simply recapitulates the myth ironically in order to undermine it.

All this is a far cry from the madcap frantic goings-on in the psychiatric clinic of *What the Butler Saw*. Orton's play owes less to the tradition of subsidised contemplation on the nation's health that the National Theatre makes possible than it does to the tradition of *Carry On* films which were thriving in the 1960s. Therefore, *What the Butler Saw*, like *The National Health*, undermines the image of the god-like and trusted doctor, but does not necessarily set out to distance itself from popular culture in the same fashion. (Although it is worth noting that in the first production of *The National Health*, the role of Barnet was taken by Jim Dale, a *Carry On* regular who appeared in *Carry on Doctor* [1967] and *Carry On Again, Doctor* [1969]) As Julia Hallam notes, the *Carry On* series was already slightly at odds with the traditional medical serial, since it sent cheeky working-class protagonists to spread havoc within the confines of the stereotypical Victorian country-manor style hospital (1997: 12). The main difference between *Carry on Doctor* and *What the Butler Saw* is, of course, the substitution of the sexually explicit for mere innuendo.

If *The National Health* is lacking in real doctors, *What the Butler Saw* suffers from a shortage of real patients. Orton admitted as much in a diary entry: 'Kenneth H. said, "In *What the Butler Saw* you're writing about madness." "Yes" I said, "But there isn't a lunatic in sight – just doctors and nurses."' (Orton, 1998) As a matter of fact, there are not even any nurses in the play, just two psychiatrists, the wife of one of the doctors, their two children (a secretary and a bellhop) and a police sergeant. We do not discover that Geraldine and Nick, the secretary and bellhop, are the children of Dr and Mrs Prentice until the concluding scene, which allows, of course, for much outrageous plot material on incest and possible incest. In fact, the play begins with Dr Prentice interviewing the naïve Geraldine for the post of secretary in his clinic, a situation he manipulates into an opportunity for seduction. Although it is clearly inappropriate in an interview, Dr Prentice manages without much difficulty to get Geraldine to strip down to her underwear. He justifies his extraordinary demand as a disinterested investigation into Geraldine's mental welfare:

PRENTICE: Never ask questions. That is the first lesson a secretary must learn. (*he pulls aside the curtains on the couch.*) And kindly remove your stockings. I wish to see what effect your step-mother's death had upon your legs.

GERALDINE: Isn't this rather unusual, doctor?

PRENTICE: Have no fear, Miss Barclay. What I see upon the couch isn't a lovely and desirable girl. It's a sick mind in need of psychiatric treatment. The body is of no interest to a man of my stamp.

(Orton, 1976: 366)

An interesting variant on 'the handsome doctor who not only cures but cares'! Before the planned seduction can progress any further, Mrs Prentice interrupts her husband and the rest of the play is a rapid spiral downwards from Dr Prentice's attempt to conceal this first indiscretion. As the play progresses, Prentice continues, with diminishing returns, to invoke the authority of his professional expertise in efforts to turn the plot to his advantage. It hardly needs to be said that there is no real doctoring done: medical science is merely simulated for the sake of expediency. The implication is that doctors, and psychiatrists in particular, are invested with a power and respect that they do not deserve and which they exploit for their own, non-medical ends. This is just about what we might expect from Orton, an iconoclast who distrusted all forms of authority (police, religious, professional) and took every opportunity available to ridicule its representatives. Furthermore, *What the Butler Saw*, like *The National Health* shares the general anti-establishment mood of the end of the 1960s. If anything, though, the play is more contemptuous of the credulous innocents who unthinkingly follow the instructions of their doctors, placing blind faith in their professional status. The play slyly asks, Why do people undress automatically when their doctors request it, when they would never do so in virtually any other circumstance?

If Dr Prentice the philanderer explodes the myth of the trustworthy and ethical medical professional in true *Carry On* fashion, then Dr Rance, his 'immediate superior in madness' (20) is the target of a more original attack from Orton's satirical energies. From the moment of his arrival in *What the Butler Saw*, Rance almost pathologically pathologises every character he encounters, providing everything from vulgar Freudian Oedipal interpretations for Geraldine's apparent mental state to a catalogue of deviancy to account for Prentice's increasingly suspicious behaviour. Prentice is, of course, only attempting to cover up his sexual indiscretions and the attendant implications for his professional status, but Rance diagnoses him thus:

> RANCE: You have under your roof, my dear, one of the most remarkable lunatics of all time. … As a transvestite, fetishist, bi-sexual murderer Dr Prentice displays considerable deviation overlap. We may get necrophilia too. As a sort of bonus.
>
> (72)

Prentice is the puppet-like character at the mercy of situation in a timebound farcical plot pattern, whereby one indiscretion by an authority figure sets rolling a snowball of confusions and complications; and in this sense *What the Butler Saw* is not radically different from a 19th century farce where the fragility of a clergyman's morality is exposed to hilarious effect. Rather more is at stake with Rance, though. Rance takes to its logical extremes the project of Prentice's clinic, as outlined by Mrs. Prentice: 'The purpose of my husband's clinic isn't to cure, but to liberate and exploit madness.' (32) The point might almost have come out of Michel Foucault's *History of Sexuality*: that psychiatry doesn't merely address and attempt to cure mental illness but by relentlessly seeking it out and sexualizing it under a scientific gaze, actually produces it as a form of knowledge (Foucault, 1978). Orton examines thereby the power invested in the head doctor, but in good Foucauldian manner, shows how the psychiatrists are not simply the subject of knowledge in a masterful sense but also implicated in the power structures produced by institutionalised knowledge: Dr Prentice's desperate situation arises from having psychiatric knowledge turned on him. What better dramatic form to explore this capacity of power than farce where characters are as much subjected to the plot as subjects of their own actions?

In summary: Nichols sets out to show us that the NHS runs is creaky, perhaps inefficient, and keeps going on a daily basis through the efforts of the ancillary staff as much as the doctors so vaunted in popular imagery as omnipotent. Orton goes one step further and addresses the power invested in the medical profession to make decisions about the health of bodies and more specifically minds (particularly in terms of sexual activity and preference). He raises to the nth farcical degree this power of making maps of subjects; sanity and madness are compartmentalized simply by virtue of a technical language and professional position. Both plays can be read as part of a general suspicion of the narratives of scientific and medical progress which doctors participate in with less and less god-given authority as we move into the 1970s.

V

My claim is that these plays are not so much *about* doctors but necessarily *feature* them because they are about the institutions to which they belong (hospitals, the medical or psychiatric establishment). If we return once more to television drama, we might ask why it is that so many of the most successful serials are based around a state institution: the television screen is full of police series, hospital series, law court dramas, army serials, dramas set in schools. To this catalogue we could easily add many situation comedies, since the milieu of this genre is so often that grand old institution for subject formation, the family. Do these institution-based dramas prevail on television because there is so much interest in the professions of their protagonists? Perhaps for a minority constituency – the members of the professions themselves – there is a tendency to compare the fictional representation with the real life profession. But I would like to suggest that for the large majority of the audience these series exist to provide fictions about those institutions which Althusser called repressive and ideological state apparatuses. It is institutions like schools, the family, the justice system, which produce subjects by inserting them into practices which they soon recognize as naturally given (Althusser, 1971). These dramas, and I include the plays of Orton and Nichols among them, fascinate audiences because it is these institutions which produce and discipline subjects and therefore are the source of ambivalence and anxiety in their viewers, anxiety which is worked through most often in the melodramatic mode. Anyone who has spent time in a hospital as a patient will know that they were hardly the protagonist of the piece. Medical drama reassures us that there are indeed protagonists within hospitals, that there are heroes and heroines within those institutions with independence and agency. In the words of Ioan Williams, they 'mediate the subjective illusion'[3]. Nichols' play sets out to show, perhaps a little heavy-handedly, how patients most certainly are not protagonists; he is not quite so sure what to do with the doctors, but *What the Butler Saw* takes the next logical step and shows the doctors to be subjects of their own power-knowledge apparatus.

Notes

1. In the same poll of the London Theatre Critics, Edward Albee's *A Delicate Balance*, Arthur Miller's *The Price* and Barry England's *Conduct Unbecoming* received two votes, and Harold Pinter's *Landscape* one.
2. See Julia Hallam, *Nursing the Image: Media, Culture and Identity*, London, Routledge, 2000 for a full development of the arguments found in this paper.
3. Professor Williams of the University of Aberystwyth used this phrase in his paper, 'Myths and Merchants' at the 'Professions in Contemporary British Drama' Conference held at the Centre for English Studies, University of London, March 6, 1998.

5   The Priest Character's Space and Function in Contemporary British and Irish Drama

Mária Kurdi

Introduction

Arguably, the character in modern drama can be defined as a complex construct, drawn from a set of experiences, to participate in the creation of an artistic reality that highlights certain aspects of the human condition and people's relationships. As semioticians maintain, characters in a play fulfil a variety of functions, categorised by them as psychological, structural and ideological (Aston and Savona, 1991: 35), both interconnected and intertwined in accordance with the unfolding dramatic roles. Among these three categories, the last one is most relevant to the issues discussed in the present paper. In my understanding, the ideological function of a character involves the political in the broadest sense, as it informs the thematic design of a particular play. On the level of dramaturgy it manifests itself in referring to or signifying through attitudes and behaviour the dominant ideas and belief systems of the social environment and historical time, their boundaries, ambivalence or confusion as the case may be. Not infrequently, their destructive effects on the individual are suggested or demonstrated by the characters' contesting, transvaluing or undermining the re-presented structures of power and related discourses. It is chiefly to establish, complicate and even reinforce this ambiguous link that the vocation, position or job of a character assumes significance in drama, assigning him or her a recognisably dual space of operation at the delicate intersection of personal sensibilities and socially prescribed orientations. Under pressure of the conflict between the private and the public spheres of life, which has been ever intensifying in the modern era, the intricate demands of professional duties and commitments as well as their manifold, often unpredictable implications tend to have a significant part in the overall politics of character construction.

In this essay I focus on the possible ideological function of clerical figures, protagonists, supporting or minor characters depending on their status, in some post-1970 texts selected from British and Irish playwriting. I will trace their mostly tension-laden connection to the existing socio-political order with its ideological constraints, and/or to the changing concept and historically evolved expectations of the priest's position in the societies of the British Isles. While doing so, I will also point to the divergent features of the cultural traditions in which these figure conceptions are rooted.

Dramatising Priests in Thatcher's Britain

David Hare's *Racing Demon* (1990), as part of the critically penetrating 'State of England' trilogy dealing with British politics and institutions, reflects on the period of Thatcherism, which has had 'the effect in this country of a huge ideological shake-out.' (Zeifman, 1992: 19) But, as the author contends, his objective was not to theorise about the conditions of the selected institutions, he merely intended 'to portray the lives of the people trying to survive in them.' (Hare, 1993: 5) *Racing Demon* offers a thorough examination of the contemporary situation of the Church of England clergy through the confrontation of characters who perceive their job in different ways and shape their attitudes and plan their actions accordingly. Its protagonist, the Reverend Lionel Espy is dedicated to doing good, working for several charity organisations and being deeply involved in community care, and he also launches a team ministry. He can be described 'as a man of conscience, rather than a man of faith' (Homden, 1995: 205), who, in the context of the allegedly divided society of the Thacherite years, becomes dual-minded over the question of how to administer to parishioners of mixed income backgrounds and concomitant needs and expectations. His groping for conviction and an alternative truth is already formulated in a private prayer that opens the play, and in his first conversation with the Bishop of Southwark: 'Our job is mainly to listen and to learn. From ordinary, working people. We should try to understand and serve them. [...] Perhaps, with time, I do find that more important than ritual.' (Hare, 1990: 3)

Although Lionel's approach is utterly humane, in so far as it advocates action instead of putting people off 'with all the cultural baggage' (59) by just talking to them, it is also an inadequate approach, as Hare himself claims, because it rests on the naive belief that everybody means good. (Zeifman, 1992: 12) Disagreeing with others does not facilitate action; in spite of all his goodwill and readiness to help the destitute, Lionel becomes isolated and, eventually, loses his present job, and thus the means to achieve his goals. His two major opponents in the drama, the Bishop of Southwark and his young curate called Tony Ferris, both consider the clergy's space in much more pragmatic terms. The former emphasises the sacramental part as a must to be observed properly for the sake of appearances: 'Give Communion. Hold services. Offer the full liturgy. And look cheerful as you do it. The people you call middle-class are entitled to that. [...] fulfil your job description. Keep everyone happy.' (4) Translating this into the language of principles, the priest's duty lies in serving the system and the conservative ideology on which that is based. The bishop's eventual dismissal of Lionel on the grounds that he has been feeding the people with his private misgivings, derives from the wish to prove that the diocese can be purified of the menace of decay and that he himself (and the conservative system he represents, one should add) has not become ineffectual. (Wilson, 1992: 210)

In contrast with Lionel, Tony is not interested in spiritual issues like the nature and value of faith, but in the Church itself, its potential and the way it can perpetuate its prescribed social role. A man of certainties, he does know what he is after: 'The statistics are appalling. We feel we've had a good Sunday if between us we attract one per cent. One per cent of our whole catchment area. [...] I want a full church.' (16) He fulfils an ideological function in the play by demonstrating how deeply the work of the clergy has been imbued with the success-oriented and business-minded spirit of the period of the 1980s. As a vicar interviewed in Hare's *Asking Around* reveals, 'The Church has got like Thatcher's government. Market forces are all.' (Hare, 1993: 37) For Tony, action is undertaken to testify to the power and efficiency of the institution in the eyes of the community. Instead of, as Lionel did, just comforting and offering friendship to Stella, a black woman in the parish who suffers from the brutal behaviour of her husband, Tony insists that she leave him and take up a charwoman's job for the church, unmindful of the cost in terms of her feeling uprooted and alienated as a result of his interference. At the same time – after openly criticising Lionel and calling him an utter failure whose 'fiddle-faddle is to leave people confused' (51) in a conversation with the other members of the team, Harry and Streaky – he is going to have supper with the bishop. The structural arrangement of these events indicates that Tony is more than ready to co-operate with the representative of power to find the best possible excuse to get rid of the colleague who ponders too much, and secure acclaim for his own victorious attitude by the same stroke.

The difference between Lionel and Tony proves to be not unlike what is suggested in Patrick Kavanagh's poem 'Father Mat,' set obviously in an Irish context, but contrasting old and new approaches with an unmistakable hint at modern dichotomies. 'Ahead of him went Power' – the contemplative old priest in the poem realises on catching sight of his young curate cycling past him, 'A man designed / To wear a mitre / To sit on committees – ' (Kavanagh in Crotty, 1995: 43). The concluding short scene of Hare's drama presents a configuration with Lionel, Tony and Frances, physically together but locked in private monologues. The woman, a lay person, stands for the spirit of transcendence, turning her head towards the sun, described as an artistic vision reminiscent of Hemingway's symbolic ending to the story *The Snows of Kilimanjaro*. The two clergymen appear to be bogged down in their narrowly conceived views. Deep in meditation, Lionel seeks an answer from God to the purpose of human suffering, whereas Tony repeats the slogans of how to revitalise the Church as a booming business and site of power: 'It's numbers, you see. [...] Once they're there, you can do anything.' (87) In spite of the divergent paths they have taken, both are characteristic products of the system that polarises people into the unhealthy extremes of feeling too much confidence or too much confusion. Their shared failure is conveyed by their common inability to harmonise the public and the private in their lives. Lionel's self-absorption alienates his wife and children, and Tony feeds his lover, Frances with a rhetoric which draws 'from the broad, shallow pool of contemporary usage' (King, 1992), instead of being sincere about their relationship.

Of the two priests completing the team ministry Harry is the one who feels close to Lionel and understands his motives. He warns Tony that his judgement of Lionel's work and contribution to the latter's humiliation, amounting to the betrayal of a friend, do damage to his conscience. However, Harry can hardly manage to defend Lionel, due to having his own problems to struggle with in a society ruled by conservative attitudes. The public impinging on the private as it does, he is filled with confusion about bringing his homosexuality into the open as his partner would prefer. His ambivalence considerably deepens when he becomes exposed to manipulative assaults from the press, which is more than eager to find and publish stories of supposedly deviant behaviour of whatever nature, and, in particular, to combat 'what they call the gay mafia.' (83). Finally, Harry leaves his job, in awareness that pretending that things are not different from what they were before the hunt began would lead to the self-demeaning state of 'succumb[ing] to the sin of despair.' (84) His departure is undoubtedly a loss to the diocese, precipitated by the morally questionable power of the media and its intricate connections with the political élite that Hare lays bare in some of his other plays written during the years of Thatcherism.

The fourth priest, Streaky embodies yet another kind of reaction to the crisis within the clergy. As an easy-going person, satisfied by the little joys of life, he does not seem to bother much about the broader moral implications of his job as long as he is not affected by a problem directly. On closer inspection, his professional approach proves simplistic, searching as it does to gain popularity by providing recipes for happiness. He prays to give thanks for what he interprets as the grace of God in a discourse which demonstrates his superficially carefree attitude: 'By my bed there's a pile of paperbacks called *The Meaning of Meaning*, and *How to Ask Why*. They've been there for years. The whole thing's so clear. You're there. In people's happiness. Tonight, in the taste of the drink. Or the love of my friends.' (56) Yet his ideological function is more complex than what Carol Homden suggests when saying that he has 'no independent life' in the drama. (Homden, 1995) In fact, he embodies the professional unwilling to fight for a cause and take risks, despite his knowledge of what may be at stake. To justify his compromise he resorts to some vague remarks dressed up in fake humanism: '[…] finally it isn't about us. […] It's about the people. […] They always have to come first.' (85). Furthermore, his inviting the just sacked Lionel to listen to old records and have a glass of wine with him back in his place to release the tension of the situation is a totally inappropriate, if not grossly insensitive, suggestion on his part.

It is Scene 8 that orchestrates the big verbal clash between the Bishop of Southwark and his subordinate, Lionel. Set in the crypt of the cathedral before the beginning of service, and having the priests wearing the outfit to match the occasion, it foregrounds the strict hierarchy that prevails within the Church. As the representative of power, Southwark arrives on the scene *'with characteristic gravity'* and attendants surrounding him. (73) The scene is tellingly introduced by the expression of his indignation at the latest piece of news, which concerns having a woman Bishop inside the Anglican Communion. A prominent functionary so shocked by change coming with the times can hardly be expected to view the nonconformist behaviour of a parish priest with understanding. Lionel becomes a victim of Southwark's conservative ambitions and shirking from anything unconventional:

You bring it on yourselves. All of you. Modernists. You make all these changes. You force all these issues. The remarriage of clergy. The recognition of homosexual love. New Bibles. New services. You alter the form. You dismantle the beliefs. You endlessly reinterpret and undermine. You witter on, till you become all things to all men. You drain religion of religion. And then you're so bound up in your own self-righteousness you affect astonishment when some of us suddenly say no.

(77)

Paradoxically, the existence of the team ministry originally devised to modernise clerical work makes it possible for the superior to sack Lionel, because the acceptance of the new system meant that individual priests could be deprived of 'their most precious right: the gift of freehold.' (Hare, 1993: 28) Southwark sacrifices a man of lower position out of fear, motivated also by the desperate need to appear efficient. On the other hand, he does not dare to engage in any more significant act to prevent or protest against changes affecting the profession on a nationwide level. His authoritarian yet also cowardly behaviour pinpoints the ramifying contradictions within the Church itself, allowing the audience to realise its ideological complicity with the conservative politics of the times (Wilson, 1992: 214), which only paid lip-service to social responsibility.

Priests in Plays Set in Colonial Ireland

Brian Friel's drama written during the years of the Troubles, partly coinciding with the Thatcherite era, shows thorough interest in the nature and operation of public discourses, among them that of the clergy, as both context and catalyst of the destructive political processes and events. *The Freedom of the City* (1973) evokes the tragic Bloody Sunday (20 January 1972), when thirteen Catholic civilians were shot dead by British soldiers. It alters historical detail, though not the basic meaning of the events, and thus gives space to Friel's keen engagement with how language influences, even constructs reality itself. The unfolding story of its three Catholic down-and-out protagonists is intersected by a range of diverse interpretations of their motives as invaders of the Derry City Hall seek refuge. F. C. McGrath's analysis points out two registers in the play's language: one of 'literary realism' portraying the victims, and the other of 'public discourse[s]' which, he continues, 'fall into at least three ideological categories – those that assume allegiance to the British government, those that sympathize with the Irish victims, and those that purport to a disinterested objectivity.' (McGrath, 1999: 101) While they are by no means of equal strategic power, all the public discourses bear some measure of responsibility for the fate of the individuals as well as for the Ulster community by setting abstractions over the truth.

One kind of distorted version of reality among the several in Friel's play is provided by a priest figure. At the opening of the play, a photographer with a flash-gun appears first beside the victims to take pictures of them. Only then does the Priest enter to administer the last rites to the dead. He follows the representatives of the media who have already appropriated a more powerful role in controlling people's lives and beliefs. Later in the play, the Priest delivers two speeches about the death of the three, the difference between which is striking. The first one is presented to his congregation, posing the question 'Why did they die?' (Friel, 1984: 125) His voluble reply represents a 'partisan view,' creating 'Christlike sacrificial martyrs' out of the three ordinary Catholics. (McGrath, 1999: 109–10) It advocates not just sympathy for the violent demise of the victims, but fabricates a story, the heroes of which have died for the dream of liberating 'their fellow citizens' from 'the injuries and injustices and indignities that have been their lot for too many years.' (125) Like the Balladeer's song which praises fighting spirit where none is actually expressed, the Priest's first speech attributes never considered goals to the trio's adventure. Both discourses develop their own agenda, fitting the mindset of the nationalist narrative but ignoring the individual side.

The second speech of the Priest in Act 2 begins with almost the same introductory words as the first one did, repeating also its question. However, the address continues in a way displaying a 'critical attitude' toward the civil rights movement that he must have assumed 'under instructions from his superiors and living up to his name.' (Andrews, 1995: 135) Deploying a carefully coded rhetoric, the Priest begins with an account of the positive aspects of the movement, then reveals its contamination by 'certain evil elements [...] with the result that it has long ago become an instrument for corruption.' (156) Again, mourning for the three victims provides an occasion for mouthing propaganda, this time of a different shade than before. Ideologically motivated as it is, the Priest's talk implies loyalty to and complicity with the British government of Northern Ireland, insofar as it indicts the acts of protest against the *status quo*. The almost complete reversal makes his discourse unusual compared with that of the other commentators, acting to suggest how Janus-faced the clergy can become under a system that shrewdly manipulates the channels instrumental to the shaping of public opinion.

In Friel's dramatic oeuvre, texts noticeably reach out to others, and most can be paired off by regarding the thematic and/or dramaturgical affinities between them. The 'pair' written later explores a new side of the complex picture, or uses a kind of lens through which to mobilise aspects of the original subject in a different historical dimension. One of Friel's Field Day plays, *Making History* (1988) has conspicuous links with *Freedom* regarding the opposition of public and private discourses, probing into the subtly interdependent issues of identity and representation in Irish culture. True to his historical role, Peter Lombard, Archbishop of Armagh, the priest figure of the *dramatis personae* is introduced in the guise of a '*church diplomat.*' (Friel, 1989: 5) He arrives on the scene bringing news from the Pope and from Spain, the allies of the Gaelic order against the political as well as religious intrusion of Tudor England. It is just the moment in Irish history that witnesses the creation of the long (to an extent still) lasting connection between Catholicism and nationalism.

Showing his *résumé*, Lombard is also the author of a work in progress, a hagiographic chronicle on the life and times of Hugh O'Neill, titled *Commentarius*. His job, as the archbishop himself describes it, is 'to tell the best possible narrative,' because of history being 'a kind of storytelling' and 'Maybe when the time comes, imagination will be as important as information.' (8–9) Friel presents a fictionalised version of history somewhat in this spirit and from the perspective of his own time, having the priest-historiographer's argumentation informed by the relevant theoretical assumptions of the twentieth century (for instance by Hayden White's ideas). Opposed to Lombard, Hugh in *Making History* expects history to present the truth about him as a split-minded Ulster leader whose private life is pervasively influenced by being raised and placed between two cultures. As a 'hybridised subject' in postcolonial critical terms, he cannot escape from the ambiguity of his in-between position whatever course of action he decides to take on whichever side.

Lombard, however, insists on rendering Hugh as the central hero of a nationalist narrative which has 'elements of myth' (67), thus making his own role comparable to that of the Four Evangelists. His 'making history' is presented as an act of public significance, offering 'Gaelic Ireland two things. [...] A hero and the story of a hero.' (67) A thoroughly secularised occupation for a clergyman, indeed, and Lombard does not hesitate to call himself 'some kind of half priest, half schemer.' (67) The equivocal description could not be more precise in regard to many more Irish priests' positions throughout history as representatives of a religion engaged in the struggle for political independence. At the time of Gaelic Ireland's anti-English participation in the Counter-Reformation movement, and throughout the centuries of failure that followed, 'historiography and poetry did the duty of political manifestos [...],' to borrow the words of historian Roy Foster. (Foster, 1989: 43)

The discursive strategy of Lombard's work bears the indelible mark of the demanding times in more than one way; the play allows us to presume that it also opposes the ambitions of the other side, manifested by the history of 'an Englishman called Spenser' (52) much treasured by the English government – for its promoting the colonialist perspective one should add. Historiography in *Making History* is inevitably subject to politics, and Lombard's *Commentarius* can be classified as 'what Bhabha calls insurgent acts of cultural translation that selectively remember and restage the past as an intervention in the present that opens up the possibility of rewriting the future.'(quoted in McGrath, 1999: 225) Hugh's individual truth, like that of many after him, falls victim to not one priest chronicler's authoritarian or arbitrary choice to treat his story the way he does, but to the widening gap between the loyalist and nationalist narratives as forces articulating the fatally diverging views on a bifurcated history.

The investigation of the role of priest characters as not only influential members of society but also as signifiers of the historically evolving ideological force of their Church(es) has continued to remain an important theme in recent Irish drama. Frank McGuinness's *Mary and Lizzie* (1989) addresses the related issues of colonial and gender oppression in pre-Famine Ireland and Victorian England. The two women protagonists incarnate the Irish mistresses of Friedrich Engels, yet their story is, again, displayed in a highly fictionalised form. A surrealist fantasy, the play utilises the trope of the journey involving encounters with real and mythical figures to throw light on the different levels of the two Irish women's exposure and resistance to, and ultimate transcendence of their particular kind of subjection to the historical condition. The third scene leads the sisters to the underworld where, under the Old Woman's (Mother Ireland's) guidance, they meet the Priest. The place is chosen with good reason: this clerical figure is a vicious mouthpiece for a new faith, serving Satan. His deformed ideas turn out to stem from the self-annihilating potential inherent in the cleavage between the warring religions of Ireland. 'This underworld magical priest represents the dualism of Catholicism and Protestantism: having united them in himself in a destructive way, he inverts both to their opposites, teaching hatred instead of love' as Csilla Bertha claims. (Bertha, 1998: 127)

'Convert and covet' (McGuinness, 1989: 9) are the key-words of McGuinness's priest-monster, summing up the spiritual and moral threat Mary and Lizzie have to face. He is also the devouring male, thus shown as an inversion of the ancient pagan goddess, in that he tries to feed on both the mind and the flesh of the sisters. The latter, however, reverse the situation and discuss eating him in a rapid Beckettian exchange of references to his bodily parts realising, as they do, 'that it is a case of destroy or be destroyed in Ireland.' (Jordan, 1997: 131) Contesting the social fixities of their time, the women, finally, triumph and force the Priest to administer to their needs – he has to perform the wedding rites for them. The acts are wholly unorthodox:

> Mary: Marry me.
> Priest: Who to?
> Mary: Myself.
> Lizzie: Marry me.
> Priest: Who to?
> Lizzie: My mother.

(13)

One wedded to herself, and the other to her (m)other, the sisters express their wish to achieve autonomous femininity and selfhood, refusing to conform to the patriarchal rules of the society inscribed in the conventional heterosexual marriage. Their possession of unity of self contrasts the fragmentation of the corrupt Priest, whose figure embodies not only the destructiveness but also the imminent failure of religion that constitutes a power contentious as well as alienating. Complicated with the issue of gender, McGuinness's work unmasks, at the same time, the narrowness of masculine politics solely governing ideological relations within a society.

John Barrett's *Borrowed Robes* (1998) further explores the contradictions related to Church and religion in early twentieth century Ireland. Through the extreme racist behaviour of its priest protagonist, the play can be seen as intimately linked to the problems piling up within the Catholic Church which, having preceded the building of the state historically, became 'a kind of surrogate state' (O'Toole, 1997: 65) during colonial times. Assuming too much power and perpetuating a centralised bureaucratic system, it also managed to facilitate the covering up of several psychologically and morally damaging incidents, resulting from the doctrine of celibacy and enforced sexual puritanism that proved to be the hotbed of various forms of aberration, perversion and child abuse. Barrett's clerical figures invite being measured against the implications of the recent scandals bringing into the open a series of 'the hypocrisies and failings which have always been present within the Church' (O'Toole, 1997: 111).

Set in 1904, the action of *Borrowed Robes* develops into the persecution of a small Jewish community of East European origin, relying on documents that uncover the responsibility of Fr John Creagh, director of a Catholic order based in Limerick, for the outbreak of the pogrom. 'It would appear,' as discussed in a major study of the Jews in Ireland, 'that the priest had been approached by shopkeepers in the city who were hostile to the Jewish pedlars because they provided unwelcome competition' (Keogh, 1998: 26–7). In his irresistible style of preaching Creagh warned people to terminate dealings with the immigrants from the pulpit, precipitating boycott then violence. (Keogh, 1998: 30) Barrett's priest figure called James Keane attacks the local Jews in a similar fashion, though the plot is conceived as fiction, introducing a complexity of ideologically and culturally entrenched personal motifs which underlie the upsurge of racism.

Keane's career is shown to have followed a typical pattern in Ireland, where many lower and middle-class parents sent a son to study for the priesthood to raise the socio-economic position and intellectual prestige of the family. Probably unfit for this career from the start and referred to by his superior, Father MacNamara as having been 'an average student, perhaps a bit below average' (Barrett 1998: 15), Keane suffers from an inferiority complex in the clerical job. Trying to make up for it, he takes the rules of the order far too rigorously, and his strong sense of duty engages him in the unrelenting pursuit of a runaway novice who has found refuge in the young Jewish widow, Sarah Levin's boarding house. Sarah and the Keane have been old acquaintances, and the attractiveness of the woman combined with her genuine concern revives his buried feelings. It is the torment of forbidden love that will dislocate him to the extent that he preaches against the object of his passion, the Jewish woman, and her race. Subject to the rules which prohibit a religious to touch and to be touched, Keane, keeping to the internalised principles, refrains from bodily contact of any kind, all the more so because of his passion. The human need for it doubly repressed in him, touching as the means to bridge the gap between self and other phenomenalises Keane's growing confusion. Seeing Sarah touch the ex-novice fuels his jealous rage for he fatally misreads the incident. The body, thus, is appropriated 'as the site of sensory interchange with its natural and social environments,' functioning to signify the ideological 'to pursue its roots in the personal' (Garner, Jr, 1994: 162).

Keane's personal crisis culminates in being torn apart between desire and duty. In private he recites from the *Song of Songs*, dreaming of the beautiful body of the beloved. Before his congregation, however, his increasingly ferocious sermons choose Sarah's people as their target: he vilifies the Jews enlarging on the economic, spiritual, and especially moral threats their presence means for the Christians. Waging the war of the flesh 'against the Spirit' as its contrary (50), he seeks new ways to advance the victory of the Spirit over the flesh when he quotes from the most biased Church literature and anti-Semitic rhetoric. Keane's preaching gains eloquence also from the energy of his repressed passion, and he proceeds to disparage otherness through its gendered materialisation: '[…] the Jewess flaunts herself in the salons of the rich – her long dark hair, her silken dress, her painted lips inviting sin. And at whom does she cast her sidelong glances? It is the Christian youth she seeks.' (58) His racist demagogy, especially because delivered by a representative of the traditionally 'rabble-rousing' priests (O'Connor, 1998: 22), is capable of catalysing the Catholics' suspicions and susceptibility to look for scapegoats in their inoffensive neighbours.

Borrowed Robes uses the Father Superior figure to give an Irishman's view of the Jews, expressed in his argument with Keane for the termination of the anti-Semitic campaign: 'You respect them, but you don't have to ask them to dinner. Very like us, though, in many ways – apart from the drink. Family centred, a strong religious sense, persecuted, forced to emigrate. I mean, basically, what is a Jew? A sober and energetic Irishman.' (38) With clichés and stereotypes in reference to both the Irish and the Jews, the speech is obliquely racist, intimating that the native identity is the norm. Emphasising uniformity rather than acknowledging the value of pluralism in culture, it extends the colonial mimicry 'as a desire for a reformed, recognizable Other' (Bhabha, 1994: 86) from one marginalised group – MacNamara's own people – to another. To complete the irony of the situation, the superior priest penalises Keane by sending him on the foreign mission, where he may as well have the opportunity to abuse yet another race.

The 'impeccably groomed' (15) and secularised MacNamara, and through him the Church itself, share a considerable amount of responsibility for the excesses of Keane's racist propaganda. When the Father Superior gives an account of how as a young priest he had himself succumbed to a sexual adventure, it shakes the young man's vocational beliefs to the core. McNamara's self-centeredness seems obvious also from the fact that following the first racist sermon, his primary concern is its potential damage to the Church's and his own reputation: 'This is my life's work, Father – trying to show them, trying to show our Protestant brethren that we can be trusted. [...] We are not Yahoos. I am Chairman of the Cultural Committee of this city!' (35) But the drama does not fail to inscribe such distortions in the larger context of colonialism that made the Irish strangers in their own land by the rule of a powerful minority. Tensions due to the authority of Britain over Irish social and cultural politics are hinted at and the bishop, who speaks with a Northern accent, answers Sarah's appeal for help claiming that 'I know very well what it's like to be ambushed on your way to school' (62). Living in a divided society that encouraged conformity had its distorting effect on all: hypocrisy in a priest, exemplified by MacNamara's behaviour, was the complex product of the need to override both the barely endurable rigour of Catholicism and the colonial subject's identity problems.

Without counter-action taken early enough, the racial aggression leads to tragedy, its self-destructiveness underscored by the violent death of a young Irishman respectful of and willing to defend the other community. In the concluding scene, victimised like Macbeth by his own victimising actions, Keane discards the 'borrowed robes' which represent clerical authority that he, undermined by his personal crisis, unforgivably misused. With its honest treatment of suffering and loss underscoring the need for a new approach from clergymen, *Borrowed Robes* joins the tendency of playwriting that reflects a 'new ethos' forming at a time, in the 1990s, when the new generation of Irish people found 'its preferred liberty in secularism, tolerance, and a new, very appealing humanism.' (Murray 1997: 246)

The closeness of Barrett's play to contemporary life is well demonstrated by the changes in its reception in Ireland during 1998 and 1999. According to the author's unique analysis of the theatrical fate of his own work, these were due to the fact that in the meantime 'there occurred a major change in Ireland in people's attitude to priests and religion itself. The clerical scandals, which had been simmering for years, finally erupted in the revelations made in three RTE television programmes under the title *States of Fear.*' As a consequence, he continues, audience sympathy for Keane at the 1999 performances eroded considerably, which the company counterbalanced by revealing more of his vulnerability. (Barrett, 2000) On the other hand, in Northern Ireland there was, again, another kind of reaction, as 'inflammatory sermons are not academic matters in the North of Ireland. These audiences were intent on the play, but quieter and less demonstrative than their Southern counterparts, and, being out of the loop of the clerical scandals, their reactions to Father Keane were far more muted.' (Barrett, 2000) In view of this, to put priests on stage in Ireland is a more controversial deed nowadays than ever before.

Dramatising Priests in Today's Ireland

Several plays set in contemporary Ireland include the figure of a priest reviewing his role in the life of a particular community, and through that the impact of faith and religion in more general terms. Dramatic modes and discourses vary as they do; the authors, nonetheless, seem equally intrigued by the question of whether or not the priest still occupies a kind of authority and moral centre in the world they recreate. The dramatic space accorded to clerical figures gives the audience a sense of their communal importance and effectiveness, but may also indicate changes in people's attitude to church-related traditions and practices.

Having spent two years studying for the priesthood, Friel retained a keen interest in how clerics as dedicated public figures watch over private lives. His artistic scrutiny, however, results in an unflattering picture. After *The Blind Mice* (1963), he 'has never again drawn a priest sympathetically for the stage. [...] In play after play the Catholic Church is held responsible for the spiritual malaise debilitating Irish society.' (Murray, 1999: XV) The priest character of *Living Quarters* (1977), Father Tom, an army camp chaplain, is as ineffectual as the canon in *Philadelphia, Here I Come!* (1964), if not more. Beginning with Sir's monologue, who claims to have been conceived in the other characters' imagination as 'the ultimate arbiter, the powerful and impartial referee, [...] a kind of human Hansard' (Friel, 1984: 178), the drama has Tom speak next, self-consciously asking Sir about his own character description. While this encounter establishes the function of the metanarrative, (McGrath, 1999: 141) it assesses Tom as 'a cliché, a stereotype' due to 'dependence' and 'excessive drinking' (180), shattering his vocational authority by the authority of self-imposed fate.

Rendered in pathetic terms, the chaplain's belated protest against the unfavourable description is already the first step of enacting what is laid down in the ledger about him: he has always failed to respond or act outside routine and in time to prevent a tragic or at least ungratifying outcome. Introduced as the close friend of a middle-class family, the Butlers, like many priests in rural Ireland, he is the only outsider figure, apart from Sir '[…] who represents the society' (180) for the family members. The irony of the fact that he turns out to be more of a parasite who preaches about 'the availability of choice and our freedom to choose' (208), yet refrains from taking responsibility, reveals the disruption of traditional bonds and relations. Embodying memory, the drama re-stages the fatal events of a particular day in the Butlers' family history, culminating in the suicide of Frank, the father, cheated by his young wife who has had an affair with his son. Individual imagination attempting to circumvent the tyranny of fact, the characters suggest various kinds of deviance from the script contained in Sir's ledger. Importantly, the chaplain is the one among them to make several such gestures, only to be mocked by the inevitable taking its course.

Tom's failure to comprehend the situation and give advice to the desperate Frank when he asks for it is followed by his sudden awakening from drunken insensitivity when his friend leaves the stage, which can be interpreted as 'a retroactive expression of his own sense of guilt' (Dantanus, 1988: 144). In contrast with the others who remain *'cocooned in their private thoughts'* (241) the chaplain is shown agitated, crying out in panic: 'You're not going to let him go, are you? You're going to stop him, aren't you? For God's sake, Ben, you've got to stop him!' (241) The detailed representation of this 'spurious concern' (242), as Sir labels it, signals Friel's critique of social and moral inertia through the grotesque helplessness of the priest character to interfere with human evil.

The priest assumes a positive role in Niall Williams' *A Little Like Paradise* (1995), a play concerned with how the aging population of Caherconn, a village situated on the Atlantic coast of County Clare, try to cope with isolation and desolation. Living on the edge of Europe, they are metaphorically 'submerged in a sea of neglect […] a periphery on the extreme peripheral and conglommered …' as Marty McInerney, their unsuccessful senator claims. (Williams in Fitz-Simon and Sternlicht, 1996: 261) In this 'place already going to the ghosts' where 'the blown and shifting quality dominates' (248) despite the presence of high technology in day-to-day transactions, the disillusioned, embittered or just bored people engage in searching for ways of self-redemption. Early in the drama Mick Maguire, a bachelor farmer enacts the ritual of death and resurrection in the pub by losing consciousness for a time and then regaining it. In the self-defined role of 'the Messenger of the Second Chance' (296), he compares himself to the archangel whose name he wears, setting the tone, as he believes, for more miracles to transpire.

Father Francis McInerney, the priest of Caherconn gives the impression of erosion itself, as he suffers from pains caused by the advanced stages of cancer, weakening not only his body but also his faith. Like the puzzled Lionel in Hare's drama, he privately speaks to God, doubting His interest in the human world where there is so much injustice and no grace for those who badly need it. His tormented monologue manifests his sense of intellectual dishonesty at the same time, on account of his inability to answer questions about the brutal victimisation of innocents: 'Why does someone kill a child? Christ! Where were you?' (273) The dramatic structure deploys parallel settings, the pub and the beach, interlacing the expression of the Father's Job-like disillusionment and God-blaming rage by the sea, with Mary's appeal to the 'Divine masters and

Universal spirits' (271) in the other part of the stage. Perusing a book of fabricated otherwordly teachings, she is keen on establishing communication with her husband who has left for America without sending any message to her about what she can expect. Juxtaposed, the incurably sick priest buried in doubts and the abandoned young woman trying to help herself by neo-pagan practices together represent characteristic problems of mankind, in face of which religious belief seems to be defunct and meaningless.

Yet the priest's fervent queries about God's existence become answered indirectly, and Caherconn does transform itself into a site of special occurrences. The needs of the community call for working miracles on a human level, as distinct from self-centered posings in the role of saints or spirits. By simply talking to the people Father Francis manages to 'keep the community together, fight superstition, build relationships, offer hope to those who have lost faith in the future' (Sternlicht, 1996: XXIII), and gains peace of mind for himself. In a lyrically inspired tone, he recalls the conditions of the birth of his much younger brother, Marty, giving new life to their appreciation for each other: 'You could hear the rosaries humming on the ceiling above. I thought you were a seagull. […] When I heard the cry. I went to the window, thought it was a gull falling or dying or something. Then I heard it again and there you were.' (281)

It is also the priest who convinces Kay, the fifty year-old widow who is in danger of marrying the wrong man, that the girl she once can be reborn to unite her with her old but faithful lover, Marty: 'Maybe she'd have a wonderful life again if you let her.' (301) When Mary spreads information of her pregnancy as a corollary of mystical experiences, Father Francis grows suspicious, but shares her happiness over this 'best possible news I could ever hear' (306) once it is said to be clinically proven. The announcement qualifies as a secular version of the Annunciation itself, as the prospect of Mary's giving life to a baby constitutes hope and promises redemption for the aging inhabitants of the village who welcome it by signs of being shaken out of their passivity and pessimism. They compete in recollecting long forgotten knowledge and forge new plans.

The Father dies in the pub surrounded by the others who by now form a community brought together in love and understanding for the celebration of a re-imagined future for themselves. His death is presented on stage by his departure to the sea, a kind of reunion with nature and finding a new shape in the great whole. Through the evocation of the mysterious links between man and the elements, reinforced by the bifocal arrangement of the stage, his words and deeds have achieved an effect that stresses the priest's function in spiritual terms, the validity of which cannot be undermined by changes in the role and influence of religion. In a seemingly god-forsaken world ruled by disadvantage and failure, God has shown His presence in the manner in which a priest, a suffering and doubt-tormented individual, can touch others and make them realise that it is their ideas and efforts that can revitalise their community and transform it into what looks and feels 'a little like paradise.' A similar miracle can happen anywhere and at any time. Williams' pertinent but not too obtrusive use of names and images borrowed from the Bible and religious narratives, exemplified by calling the priest figure Father Francis, results in coalescing the human and the supernatural, offering their unity as an alternative to despair and losing the hope that things may take a different turn.

Martin McDonagh also places his priest character in an off-centre setting, the West of Ireland, but as a helpless witness. The author's subversive approach results in both a ruthless and unsentimental picture of this part of the country, questioning its status as serving a long held national 'metaphor of social cohesion and an earnest of the cultural unity that transcended class politics and history.' (Brown, 1990: 92) Several playwrights have been in this terrain before him, so one hardly wonders why heritage challenges McDonagh. He re-inscribes character types primarily of Synge's drama, their ideological and psychological functions shown in parodistic terms. In the first parts of *The Leenane Trilogy, The Beauty Queen of Leenane* (1996) and *A Skull in Connemara* (1997), the claustrophobic world of Leenane is festering with mean conflicts and hatreds, where selfishness and brutality testify to the obvious lack of spiritual guidance. Recalling *The Playboy of the Western World*, the priest of the community remains an off-stage figure. However, whereas the similarly positioned Father Reilly of Synge embodies an authority held in some, even if conventionally understood, respect, McDonagh's Father Welsh cuts a ludicrous figure, by no means a 'moral voice' any more. (Merriman, 1999: 314) Signalling his loss of identity and voice of authority, his family name is repeatedly mistaken for Walsh by the other characters, a running joke through the trilogy.

With his spiritual influence both declining and rejected, the first two plays contain references to the priest, almost exclusively, in contexts which associate him with material interests, intellectual impoverishment or physical violence. Ray, the youngest character in *The Beauty Queen*, is a keen watcher of television, escaping from boredom and the emptiness of his own life, to the excitement that impersonal media consumption can provide. Most likely the television shows and not his real needs inspire him to wish to learn to drive and buy the second hand car that Father Welsh/Walsh is selling. To the priest's dubious credit, Ray's description of him asserts that he 'seldom uses violence, same as most young priests. It's usually only the older priests go punching you in the head.' (McDonagh, 1996: 9) In *Skull*, the protagonist, Mick Dowd's job is to dig up skeletons in the churchyard and dispose of them so that new graves can take the place of the old ones. The priest, like the guards, is implicated in the enterprise and it is probably not for unselfish reasons that he promises Mairtin, the young halfwit of the village a nice sum of money to help Mick do the work and keep an eye on him at the same time. With the skeletons old secrets come to light, and the offstage priest seems eager to profit from sharing the information with the other authority figures, through which means he may hope to regain importance in the eyes of the people.

It is in *The Lonesome West* (1997), the third part of the trilogy that Father Welsh appears as an onstage character of the Leenane world. Shattering the myth of the West from many angles, including religion, the community in the play is one where brutally committed crimes are followed by the suicide of the ineffectual guard. The traditional value of Catholicism is interpreted by Coleman, one of the brother protagonists, who is the murderer of their father: 'It's always the best ones go to hell. Me, probably straight to heaven I'll go, even though I blew the head off poor dad. So long as I go confessing to it anyways. That's the good thing about being Catholic. You can shoot your dad in the head and it doesn't even matter at all.' (McDonagh, 1997: 53–4). Valene, the other protagonist collects cheap figurines of saints out of habit, which his brother can hardly wait to destroy. In these circumstances, Father Welsh cannot but desperately repeat the clichés of religion without any tangible effect, and his frustrated efforts to reform people leave him thoroughly depressed. The welling up of his self-doubts are, in a grotesque reversal of social roles, contextualised and judged by the parricide brother: 'The only thing with you is you're a bit too weedy and you're a terror for the drink and you have doubts about Catholicism. Apart from that you're a fine priest. Number one you don't go abusing pure gasurs, so, sure, doesn't that give you a head-start over half the priests in Ireland?' (7) Horrified by the brothers' open expression of hatred and violence, he reacts in a pathetic way when deliberately scalding his clenched fist by dipping it in the molten plastic figurines steaming in a bowl on the stove. Yet his fragile mock-sacrifice fails to shock or even move, let alone transform anyone. Leenane qualifies as 'the murder capital of fecking Europe' (34), as Welsh concludes; it is a comment all the more pointed because of the reference to the EC in the play.

The Leenane world, however, is not unequivocally rotten. Love and tenderness are not absent from it. In Scene 4 Father Welsh and Girleen, the pretty but frivolous daughter of the publican, a graceless version of Synge's Pegeen, sit together and almost agree that happiness can be considered as the goal of human life. At home in the world of popular culture spread by the media but without finding the means to communicate private needs and desires, her emotions for him remain concealed in incomplete gestures. On the other hand, the man of the Church is barred from pondering the prospect of a self-renewing relationship with the girl by duty and custom, and he chooses suicide to terminate his private misery and also redeem the devastating moral vacuum of his parish. His letter of farewell to the brothers appeals to their innate goodness and ability to forgive and love each other, in a faint imitation of St Paul's teachings about Christian living. After renewed fraternal collisions, Valene almost burns the priest's letter, then pins it back onto the crucifix, making it part of an ornament displayed out of custom, though neglected, as brutality continues to dominate the brothers' lives.

McDonagh reveals mindless self-destructiveness as the underside of rural life, but the postmodern strategy and black humour he deploys refuse to encourage the audience to interpret this chaos as a truthful representation of Irishness. Rather, it constitutes a kind of anti-pastoral that exposes by exaggeration the still lurking colonial distortions (like child molestation by priests, mentioned with special emphasis), conflated with the alienating influences of the present. Father Welsh in *The Lonesome West* has lost meaningful contact with his flock amidst the godlessness of the Leenane microcosm where religion has ceased to be a spiritual power. However, with its absurdities, McDonagh's construction of this character underscores not only the threatening decline of faith but also the dissolution of familiar communal bonds in a world where local values and customs may erode under the negative effects of globalisation.

Conclusion

The few priest characters surveyed in the present essay have been selected with the intention of suggesting the richness of dramaturgical challenges inherent in the representation of individuals practising this profession in Britain and Ireland. *Racing Demon* is unique in offering a panoramic though remarkably concentrated view of a group of clerics' attitudes at a given moment in the social history of Britain. The priest as character has more currency and variety in Irish drama for the well known reason that religion has been a component of the national identity for centuries. Hare's approach, however, would be barely viable there, because the range of complexities involved in the subject of the Irish clergy as such could not be contained by the structure of one work. 'The contemporaneity of the national present,' as Bhabha says of postcolonial cultures, 'is always disturbed by another temporality' (Bhabha, 1994: 143), and in most plays conceived in Ireland recently the past is evoked either as part of the historical consciousness or through the interrogation of the social, psychological and cultural tensions of the present. Rather than charting a particular section of society, Irish drama, often through non-realistic means, tends to oscillate within the larger terrain of cross-communal interchanges, complicating thus the function of the priest characters beyond the bounds of discernable conditions. Nevertheless, the clerical figures in both the British and Irish plays discussed here share the common feature that their multivalent relations to power, discourses and traditions highlight several other aspects, constraints, deficiencies as well as possibilities, of the worlds in which they are situated.

6   The Depiction of the Artist in David Storey's *Life Class*: The Play as Visual Art

Stephen Di Benedetto

There is a tradition within painting of self-portraiture – the artist depicting himself in the midst of his work. Think of any of Vincent Van Gogh's self-portraits, with his eyes staring intently at the viewer, while he holds paintbrushes sticking in his hand. The furrows of painted texture and colour make manifest his passion and torment. Theatre too can be an expressive art form that leads viewers to consider the artist at work. David Storey, both a playwright and a visual artist in his own right, uses the medium of the theatre to depict an artist at work in his studio. Rather than being confined to rendering his subject with pigment or marble, Storey is able to use bodies, movement and words. In *Life Class*, he depicts a professional artist at work to create a metatheatrical event that suggests the ways in which spectators look at visual art can be applied to the ways in which they look at plays. In this way, he not only captures the semblance of the artist, but also the experience of the type of work that the artist purports to create. The theatrical presentation is a sensory experience of the conditions of the artist's life class for the sake of the spectators.

Cultural and artistic influences

Storey is best known as a novelist and a playwright, but he only came to writing after studying to be a fine artist. He was born in 1933, to a Yorkshire mining family. He has held a variety of jobs ranging from professional footballer, to schoolteacher, to marquee erector. He is both an award-winning novelist and playwright, most prominent during the 1960s and 1970s[1]. Though now in retirement, his work is still in the public eye: his play *The Changing Room* was revived by the Royal Court in 1996; his novel *A Serious Man* was published in 1998; and a new collection of his plays was published by Methuen in 1999. As a young man he refused a scholarship to attend Reading University to become a schoolteacher as his parents wished, opting instead to attend Wakefield Art School in the early fifties. Later, with the money he earned from a rugby-league contract, he was able to attend The Slade School of Fine Art in London from 1953–1956, studying under Tom Manning on weekdays and working as a Rugby League player in the Industrial North at the weekend.[2]

The influence of his training and development is useful for understanding the ways in which he creates plays. Storey excelled at the Slade, winning a Summer Composition Prize in October 1954, a book prize at the Steer Prize submission, and a travelling award in 1955. In March of 1955 Lawrence Gowing said of Storey's work that it was the best of the top row (Chaplin, 1986). Even though he had won these accolades for his figurative painting at the Slade, in his final year Storey became 'frustrated by the two-dimensional element of painting and began working on constructivist pictures incorporating plaster of Paris and metal objects onto the picture surface' (Anon, 1994). His instructors did not believe this three-dimensional work had any merit and chastised him for his efforts. These frustrations with the limitations of painting led him to abandon it.

Storey then began working as a novelist, and although he did not pursue the fine arts, his interest in its aesthetic continued to shape his depiction of the world, as is evident from the many striking visual images his novels and plays contain. These images bring alive the world in which the characters live. They are reminiscent of the free-flowing emotion of the gestural techniques used by Frank Auerbach and Leon Kossoff, prominent painters of the time who were said to influence Storey (Snow, 1996). Storey uses prose to create a sort of literary gesturalist expression in Pasmore:

> The houses themselves had been quite small, formless, almost without shape. Now most of them had been restored. White, gleaming fronts confronted each other across narrow streets, or, in the case of the square, overlooked the cultivated patch of the central gardens.
>
> (Storey, 1976: 19)

These images are expressive in themselves. Furthermore, the gesturalist technique of using darkness and weight for background and bright colours to highlight the emotions emanating from the figure also finds its way into Storey's prose (again in *Pasmore*):

> Even now he couldn't help but think that, whatever his present circumstances, the outcome would inevitably be for the good. The gloom was only there to emphasise the light. He only thought he was going mad during those moments when his distractions could find no other relief.
>
> (1976: 23)

As Martin Price comments, the visual image 'never departs from the circumstantial detail that we expect of realism, but never gives us the amount of detail we seek ... the result is a series of events that are almost obsessive and almost hallucinatory' (1974: 557). This hallucination renders a picture as full of emotional distortion as any by Kossoff or Auerbach. Storey capitalises on this type of imagery not only to depict the action, but also to depict the emotional state of the character.

John Stinson points out, 'The landscape generally mirrors the psychic climate of the characters, at times one landscape will symbolically contrast with another, especially city/ country, to highlight Storey's dualistic themes' (1977: 142). Storey uses on this type of imagery to get at the complexity of Radcliffe's overwhelming emotional conflict:

> By some mysterious orientation the sun was now shining directly at the northern flank of the Place and therefore straight into his window. It was a white ball of rabid intensity set against a smooth and impenetrably black sky. White drops fell from its phosphorescent interior, draining against blackness until they touched the earth in luminous explosions … . The next moment, it seemed the Place itself spun around, swung ponderously on some central pivot of stone.
>
> (1965: 232)

The spatial environment of the Place becomes the apparatus for conveying Radcliffe's mental state. As is common with novels, the text lets the reader feel the perceptions as much as describing the perspectives. This use of gestural imagery as a pathway to observing the emotional landscape of the characters finds its most economical use in Storey's plays.

Years later when Storey began producing his plays he found that 'playwriting emerged from the constraints he felt as a painter' (Anon, 1994: 23). He relates it 'had something to do with the proscenium arch. I felt aesthetically excited by it. There was a three-dimensional element; you can go up and down, in and out' (Anon, 1994: 23). The theatre seems to have given him a ground where he could render his spatial vision using both figural techniques and three dimensions.

For Storey, the move to theatre was a synthesis of his novelist's prose and painterly vision. Storey, after a period of writing for his novel, would find he could write a play: 'On a slow day with the novel, he would find another play spring fully formed into his head' (Anon, 1976: 35). He has a skill for producing a finished product with few changes; all his plays are written in less than five days. He told the *Sunday Times* that 'he had lately turned to painting again, at moments of despair' (Anon, 1976: 35). The successful composition of his plays is 'thanks partly perhaps to his experience of painting, he could form in his mind a three-dimensional image of how the interrelationships might be brought to physical realisation' (Hayman, 1973: 11–12). The theatre seems to have given him a ground where he could render his vision using both figural techniques and three dimensions. His painterly theatrical vision is a natural synthesis of his development as a painter and as a prose writer. Art and artists can be found in many of his fictional worlds. For example, characters from his novels *Radcliffe* and *A Prodigal Child* both dabbled in art. There is Andrew, from his play *In Celebration* who gave up a law practice to become a painter; there is Gordon the industrial design teacher/ illustrator in his novel *Flight into Camden*; and of course, there is Colin Freestone, the art teacher from his novel *A Temporary Life* (the model for his play *Life Class*).

The play as visual expression

In general, critics lump *Life Class* into a category with *The Contractor* and the *Changing Room*, which they define as Storey's 'plotless' plays. There are three significant articles that address the role of the artist in Storey's work: Ruby Cohn's 'Artists in Play' (1992); Susan Rusinko's 'A Portrait of the Artist as Character in the Plays of David Storey' (1989); and William Hutchings' 'David Storey's Aesthetic of 'invisible events'' (1992). They approach *Life Class* with the perspective of the ways in which the themes in the play are essential to understanding what Storey believes to be the role and task of the artist and art in society. Hutchings, in particular, suggests that its thematic statements 'concern *how* the play is to be understood … rather than specifically what the action of the play means' (1992). He sees it as a statement instructing spectators to understand the play as 'uneventful' rather than as an 'invisible event'. In other words, instead of thinking of the plays as without plot, the 'central action is the formation and dissolution of a collective bond as his characters are united – though *only temporarily* – through a common purpose and a shared endeavour.' Spectators are shown how to appreciate the beauty of the ways in which characters interrelate in the process of bringing about an event like the construction of a tent or the drawing of a picture.

Hutchings' ideas can be taken even farther. The play is more than just a theatrical invisible event; it is a work of visual art that can be understood as a series of still lives. Installation art is a useful illustration of the aesthetic effect of Storey's depiction of work environments. Nicholas De Olivera, Nicola Oxley and Michael Petry define installation as a term 'to describe a kind of art making which rejects concentration on one object in favour of the relationships between a number of elements or of the interaction between things and their contexts' (1996). *Life Class* asks the spectators to look at the theatrical medium as they would look at a piece of visual art. Instead of merely looking at a static image as they would with a painting or sculpture, they can look at many images made up of figures interrelating in space. The play becomes a series of relationships between objects that operate as dramatic expression.

Storey uses the dramatic medium in *Life Class* to depict an artist, Allot, at work. He teaches a life study class at a provincial Northern technical college, where he must help aspiring artists learn to draw from nature. Allot pontificates an aesthetic philosophy that revolves around the 'invisible event'. This 'invisible event' according to Allot, is something that takes place when spectators watch the minute and seemingly mundane interactions of life transpire. Throughout the first act no dramatic action of any note takes place. The immediate task at hand is to set up the easels and draw the posing nude model – his eight sophomoric students, belch, burp and lewdly joke their way through the day as they draw. These characters are Storey's expressive medium.

The different trends in art practice and theory during the 1950s and 1960s are shown through various characters' idiosyncratic behaviour. Allot's students are poor disciples of the avant-garde. Each practises a range of method that was being experimented with at the time. Saunders uses plumb-lines and grids: 'Look at all those plumb-lines … . Anybody'd think he was going to reconstruct me … build me in concrete somewhere else' (he sounds like he uses Coldstream's methods) (Storey, 1980, 187). Catherine, without a mark on her paper, claims she was 'pin-pointing the principal masses' (184). Warren breaks the drawing into its principal masses and is described as 'Crushing it to bloody death, it seems to me. (*Turns the drawing upside down.*) The Black Hole of Calcutta … See it?' (189). Their techniques are a run-down of so-called methods of composition. Each character displays a method illustrative of stylistic trends in visual arts. Even the headmaster Foley wants Allot to set a classical pose for them to draw, not some 'straight up and down nonsense' (190). Allot advocates the more radical departure from the traditional constraints of fine art practice. Rather than copy the conventions of traditional culture, he suggests that new aesthetic compositional principles should be put into practice – that is to say, he embraces the notions of the fluxus artists and the happening artists of the late 1960s and 1970s. These artists moved art out of the traditional museums and used simple actions or created environments as activities or sites of art.

Life Class remains within traditional dramaturgical constraints, yet Storey applies these contemporary avant-garde principles to the depiction of the artist at work. Beyond the frame of the proscenium arch is the stage setting of the play. The playscript describes it as:

> A Stage. Off-centre, stage right, is a wooden platform, some six to eight feet square, on castors. Beside it are two metal stands, about six feet high, each equipped with vertical flat-plane heaters. Scattered around the platform are two or three easels and several wooden 'donkeys': [these are] low, rectangular stools with an upright T-shaped bar at one end. On one, folded, is a white sheet. There are two hessian screens, one upstage centre, the other centre left. Upstage left is a rack with coatpegs.
>
> (153)

Though the specific placement of the set pieces is probably taken from Jocelyn Herbert's design for the first production, all of the components are used during the course of the play. These items must be present in the on-stage environment. Added to this image are characters and the props they carry on with them. Spectators are presented with a picture of artists in the activity of drawing. What makes this staging different from other plays is that very little else happens during the play. Storey stages these images so spectators can look through his lens at his depiction of the gathering of students studying art. The characters inhabit the stage environment, which is a dilapidated art studio. Characters go on and off stage throughout. Other teachers come in for cups of tea, the model poses and takes a break, and students go in out for no particular reason (Bent, 1996).

The processes that spectators carry out to analyse this type of performance can be described with an example from fine art. Richard Brilliant describes the traditional function of the group portrait in painting:

> In Dutch group pictures, the integrated ensemble may prevail over the independent individual, but in them the strong emphasis on the realistic depiction of specific individuals permitted each person's portrait to compete for close, if momentary, visual and psychological attention. The Dutch artists seemed to compel the viewer's eye to move from face to face, never losing sight of the others in the contemplation of the one. Such works are peculiarly cooperative and collusive in their nature, because each person in the group contributes to, and draws from, the presentational dynamic of the whole.

Some conformity to the norms of the group, whatever these might be, affects all members, forcing each person to evince some significant degree of participation as a way of manifesting the alleged coherence of the group, as represented in the work of art.

(1991: 93)

Brilliant's analysis of Dutch group pictures describes the synergistic characteristics of individual portraits competing for focus, where this competition only serves to emphasise the nature of the whole over the individual. In viewing a group portrait, the spectator gets a fleeting impression of each member's personality. Focus shifts between the different figures, and thereby the spectator is furnished with a general impression of the whole composition. Theatre naturally does this as an action unfolds over the duration of the play through the actions or range of characters. Storey's playtext directs the spectators' focus through the tolerances and parameters implicit within its dramaturgical structure. [i] Playwrights create visual rhetoric using the semiotic systems available through production. Their writing implicitly and explicitly manipulates conventions to guide practitioners in their staging of the play. Parameter and tolerance are made tangible by the requirements of the play's action. If the action demands that ink be spilled, then it will be spilled. The images in themselves are mundane, however, it is the accumulations of these experiences that creates the event of the play. The characters fill their time with adolescent flirting, joking and showing off:

CATHERINE: You ought to see what he's drawn, Jilly.
BRENDA: Better not.
WARREN: Cop a handful of them each evening.
GILLIAN: Shut your mouth.
WARREN: Tits the size of Windsor Castle. [*Standing, peering over.*] Cor blimey ... get the Eiffel Tower between two o' them.
MOONEY: Piss off.
BRENDA: [*To Warren.*] Upset him.
MOONEY: Piss off you as well.

(pp. 175–6)

Jokes about anatomy, physical flirtation, and comments about the model undressing all contribute to an atmosphere degrading to women. Occasionally, their conversation drifts from gossip and speculation towards more serious matters of art and life, such as why are there not more famous women artists. As with the other plays, the characters' plausibility is not as important as what their presence adds to the whole of the play. Allot even says something of that nature, 'It's merely a question of seeing each detail in relation to all the rest ... The whole contained, as it were ... in a single image. Unless you are constantly relating to the whole ... a work of art cannot exist'. It is the interrelationship of all of the elements of drama that culminate in the 'event' of the play. The result of all this activity is the creation of moving sculptural images for spectators to watch. Characters stand close as they talk of something intimate. Or they touch to flirt and move apart:

[Matthews] grapples with [Brenda]: takes her.

BRENDA: Get off! … Get on! … Get *off*!
CARTER: Here. Here. Here. What's going on in here? […]
MATHEWS: She's molesting me, Kenneth … . Ever since I came in … . Follows me
           around. Just look.

*Having been released by Mathews at Carter's entrance, Brenda has followed him around to hit him
back; now, however, she moves off.*

(156)

This seemingly innocuous behaviour sets up the atmosphere of the play, which by
today's standards could be described as one of sexual harassment. They put on
clothing and take off clothing:

*[Catherine … takes off gloves. Brenda has disengaged herself from Carter: she crosses over to
Catherine.]*

BRENDA: Did you bring it with you?
CATHERINE: Here, then; have a look.

[She gets a hat from the straw bag; tries it on for Brenda's approval].

(158)

Or they sit down and stand up. These ever-changing interrelationships of figures give
spectators an impression of the space, an impression of the activity of drawing, and an
impression of the characters that inhabit the space. A phantom climax of the play
comes in the second act, when the model is seen to be raped. It is not entirely clear if it
occurs or if it is just staged as a gag by the students, but Allot makes no effort to stop
it. Because of his aesthetic principle, he does not intrude on this invisible event. Rather,
he believes that the seeds of ideas that are generated by the event will blossom in some
untold creation. Allot did not regulate the sexually charged atmosphere of the
classroom, because he was waiting to see what happened. However, his inaction was
deemed as action when the administration terminated his contract.

Art is more important than the product, so it is the artist's task to influence his
medium – whether it is pigment or the atmosphere of an environment. To Allot, art
takes place in the mind as an inwardly conscious event. In the artistic process, it is not
the product that is the key, but the act of observing and exerting an influence over
something. He tells one of his students:

The problem, Catherine … isn't to pin-point … nor even to isolate … it's to incorporate
everything that is happening out there into a single homogeneous whole … . There's a
great deal happening … . Not in any obvious way … nevertheless several momentous
event are actually taking place out there … . Subtly, quietly, not overtly … but in the way

that artistic events *do* take place ... in the great reaches of the mind ... the way the leg, for instance, articulates with the hip, the shoulders with thorax; the way the feet display the weight ... the hands subtended at the end of either arm ... . These are the wonders of creation.

(184–5)

Allot advocates that the artist must observe everyday human interaction and then incorporate it into a piece of visual art. In a recent introduction to the play, Storey comments that the students

> Have found their way into what might be described as his allegorised arena (i.e., on his 'canvas') – a phenomenological act, and perception, which Allot concludes, is, like all art, expressive – an embodiment – of his time.

(Storey 1998: xii)

Allot has given up painting and drawing. To him, just to experience or to influence what is going on around him in a room is art. The aim of the creative process, that is to say the subject of art, is not just to leave something on canvas, but to be a part of the total experience. To illustrate this point, another student, Mathews offers to model so that Allot can draw him. Mathews assumes a pose and Allot draws on the pad in front of him. After Allot is done he leaves the room and Mathews talks with another teacher:

MATHEWS: First time I've seen his drawing.
PHILLIPS: One of the leading exponents of representational art in his youth, was Mr Allot ... you'd have to go back to Michelangelo to find a suitable comparison ... .

[*Mathews stoops over pad: peers closely.*]

MATHEWS: There's nothing there ... .
PHILIPS: Now of course ... an impresario ... purveyor of the invisible event ... so far ahead of his time you never see it.
MATHEWS: I've been posing there for half an hour!

(p. 216)

As Philips explains, Allot applies his artistic talents to his pursuit of an avant-garde ideal that art is more than the product that is created. Such practices are not received well because the intended viewers are not accustomed to seeing the world in this way. When Allot returns, Mathews inquires about the drawing

MATHEWS: I was just looking at the drawing, sir.
ALLOT: There isn't any drawing ... or, rather, the drawing was the drawing ... perhaps you weren't aware.

(p. 219)

The event is the thing and its product is only incidental. The artist's act is contained in the experience of the act of creation. In other words, the artist's mediation and processing of the creative act is the artistic experience; nothing else matters. Allot observed the physical motion of drawing what he saw, except that he did not use any medium to record the movements of his hands. The students never see Allot practising the techniques he professes and rumours abound about what he produces. Catherine finally asks:

> CATHERINE: What sort of paintings do you paint, sir?
> ALLOT: I don't.
> CATHERINE: Do you do sculpture, then?
> ALLOT: No.
> CATHERINE: What do you do, then, sir?
> ALLOT: It's my opinion that painting and sculpture, and all the traditional forms of expression in the plastic arts, have had their day, Catherine … . It's my opinion that the artist has been driven back – or driven on, to look at it in a positive way – to creating his works, as it were, in public.
>
> (p. 188–9)

The product of art is not the production of a material object for private perusal, but a transient event meant to be experienced. Here Allot describes what is essentially a 'happening' – that is to say, a fine art practice of creating a controlled environment for spectators to enter and in which they can participate. The ways in which the event transpires depends upon the reactions of the participants to the stimuli. Art becomes a lived, phenomenological experience guided by the constraints of the form of the event.

Whether an invisible event can constitute an artistic product is interrogated as well. Towards the end of Act I, Philips asks if he has figured out how to sell his artwork, but Allot has not yet determined that (202). Perhaps Storey has. He brings spectators into the theatre to watch his transient composition, otherwise understood as a play, be recreated each evening according to his plans that exist in the form of a playscript. Allot elucidates the process in another conversation with Catherine:

> Just as Courbet or Modigliani, or the great Dutch Masters … created their work out of everyday things, so the contemporary artist creates his work out of the experience – the events as well as the objects – with which he's surrounded in his day-to-day existence … for instance, our meeting here today … the feelings and intuitions expressed by all of us inside this room … are in effect the creation – the re-creation – of the artist … to the extent that they are controlled, manipulated, postulated, processed, defined, sifted, refined … .
>
> (188)

Allot explains that he is the one in control of the events in the classroom, but Storey is the real artist who has created a play that requires the actors to behave and say certain things. This is metatheatrical contemplation on the ways in which writers create and control artistic expression. The play is the playwright's piece of visual art whose creation is revealed in performance. Storey's control is manifest in subtle ways; what goes on stage depends on what needs he has for the characters. Catherine leaves the stage to fill her pen, Mathews and Gillian dance together, and Allot critiques the students' efforts at drawing. As stated previously, the ways in which they draw is based on their peers' comments in the dialogue as implicit tolerances and parameters. Spectators are presented with what looks like a naturalistic play, but like *trompe l'oeil* painting – it only is perceived as naturalistic. They do not learn anything concrete about the characters or their background as one might in a naturalistic play. The ambiguity of the actions and the images leaves the composition open to interpretations by the actors, directors and spectators, thereby offering a range of possibilities in which to engage with the experience. How did Allot arrive at his aesthetic? Does Allot commit suicide after he is fired for the rape? Does he ever paint again? We do not know and the play will never tell us. It may be that Storey does not know himself. The play becomes a riddle for the spectator to consider and project opinions. It is an artist's depiction of the ways in which he sees a life class and the ways in which the characters behave, interact and occupy that space. The event is the feelings and intuitions that the theatre spectator experiences while watching the playwright's work performed. Seeing that unfold is the act of watching the creative processes of an artist.

The techniques used to portray this life class are similar to the principles that Allot advocates for perceiving and understanding art as distinct from life. By watching the physical movement of the actors through the stage environment, such as when the students sit quietly observing Stella as they draw, and listening to the aesthetic philosophy of its protagonist when he outlines the invisible event, the spectator is confronted with images of artists at work. While watching this depiction, one can begin to question the visual mechanisms that are at work in its presentation: 'Why am I watching actors observing a nude model?' Like the avant-garde practices in the visual arts during the 1970s, the playwright creates an artwork that is concerned with the act of watching. It is self-reflexively contemplating its theatrical form. It shows what it is, the ways in which it is what it is, but leaves what it all means to the reception of the spectator. In this case the spectators are students being asked to consider their part in this creative process. It is the way in which the spectators see what they see that constitutes the artistic event.

Viewing theatre and viewing art are two separate experiences, yet they share many common traits. Recently, under the auspices of the 'Live art mailing list', artists have been struggling to define the hybridization of art and theatre. These discussions can help illuminate the experimentation that Storey was undertaking in the late 1970s. Michael Blass identified one reason why hybrid forms remain on the margins of performance:

> In theatre … it is rather important that 'things happen'. Otherwise you get bored just sitting there in rows in the dark. In a gallery, you're not disappointed when 'nothing happens' … As soon as you start crossing the borders between these different ways of viewing art, expectations can be confused. A 'theatre person' expects to watch something, a 'visual art person' expects to look at something. Live performance that 'follows the

rules' of visual art can be pretty dull, unless you start looking at it actively instead of watching it passively. This means that the expectations of the public before they come are in practice very important … it's important that they expect to look, not watch, even though there are many live elements.

(1997)

The playwright as an artist, structures those live elements in hopes the viewer can perceive a range of ideas as they see interactions and hear dialogue. The principles that Storey uses to build his compositions are one possible way of merging expressive forms to communicate to spectators. He uses aesthetic techniques of the visual arts to construct hybrid theatrical compositions. Storey's perception offers a framework or method of organization with which to break down spatial / visual components to construct a play with a visual spine. He creates a dramaturgical structure that takes advantage of visual components to keep in play a range of possibilities that are not always expressed best through text alone. As our culture becomes more and more reliant upon visual means, alternative methods of creation and spectatorship will become more prevalent and will have to be taken into account.

Life Class is about the activities these students and teachers carry out each day. It asks the spectator to look at daily life as constructed by the playwright and watch the minute and seemingly mundane for all that is happening there, whether seen or unseen. Stephen Bent, who played Warren in the 1974 production, liked the idea that Storey might be painting with people:

Ah, that's a very good way of putting it. Is that blob in the corner a person, or is that bold stroke in the left-hand corner an act? It is like painting with people and it almost becomes a dance as well. In *Life Class* people go on and off stage throughout. Other teachers come in for cups of tea, and students are going out for no particular reason. It just moves around in a circle.

(Bent, 1996)

After watching this dance of three-dimensional painting, the spectators are left to consider what they saw. It is a process of leaving questions unanswered in the end. It is exactly in the vein of the expressionists to render visible through artistic means what is invisible and felt.

Integrated systems of expression

Storey's work is a filter between realist theatre and the coterie expressions of avant-garde happenings. We are offered a picture of a recognisable world with a chance of finding our own path and concrete reaction to a work of art. Quigley sums up the strength of Storey's drama:

Is not in the solutions it offers but in the subtlety and variety of the perspectives it provides on the dilemmas inherent in social contracts and social commitments. And the foundation of that dramatic strength is not a simple reliance upon inherited devices, but the utilisation of emblematic structures and settings of striking originality.

(1979: 276)

Storey claims the plays write themselves. As the text grows, the image is given a more elaborate explanation. The playwright's process is much like the spectators' process – images slowly emerge and clarify themselves. Once the tracks are laid out, the spectators can contemplate the action of the play in retrospect and define why they responded the way they did to the play.

Storey's plays are an integration of fine art principles with text created to capture in three dimensions over time the atmosphere of spatial environments as experienced by its inhabitants. He uses the theatrical form to create a flow of images. These images are filled by the activities of daily life and animated by the rhythms of the characters that move through them. While his plays appear to be naturalistic, the activities and language build a complex emotional atmosphere. The space becomes the subject of the composition, rather than the context of the composition. Conversely, the human activities and conversation provide the context with which to view the space.

Storey uses the theatre as an outlet for expression that is beyond the capabilities of the traditionally conceived constraints of the fine arts and the constraints of prose fiction. The theatre provides him with a malleable medium that can balance language, image and movement. This forum can depict an environment and also provide an emotional perspective; spectators can both see and feel the space as they would outside of the artistic context. Bent put it best when he stated that the spectators have to take an active part in the plays, because Storey 'leaves a lot of things up to the audience. It is up to you to decide what the history was, why the character is like that, or what bad experience made him that way. It is criminology watching these plays' (Bent, 1996).

All successful playwrights have a sense of spatial awareness. They all use techniques that best serve their chosen expression. Visual stimulation is something we all deal with from birth. Spectators are visually literate in that they can read culturally constructed proxemic behaviour. On a daily basis, the average human is bombarded with visual stimulation from mass media. Throughout his career Storey's work has challenged preconceived notions of spectatorship by striving to find the best mode of expression to render his vision of the world. He has reacted to critical misunderstanding of his plays and attempted to teach spectators the ways in which his works can be viewed. As spectators become more aware of the visual world of his work, the clearer the abstract arguments about class and social hierarchy will become.

Notes

1. Among his awards for fiction are the Macmillan Fiction Award (1960) for *This Sporting Life*, the John Llewellyn Rhys Memorial prize (1963) for *Flight in Camden*, the Somerset Maugham Award (1963) for *Radcliffe*, the Faber Memorial Prize (1976) for *Pasmore*, and the Booker Prize (1976) for *Saville*. His plays *The Contractor*, *Home* and *The Changing Room* each won the New York Critics Best Play of the Year Award.
2. His article 'Journey Through a Tunnel', in *The Listener*, 1 August 1963, pp. 159–61, reflects on his days travelling back and forth by train to Wakefield.

7 The Artist as Character in Contemporary British Bio-Plays

Daniel Meyer-Dinkgräfe

Since the considerable commercial and critical successes of *Piaf* by Pam Gems in 1978 and Peter Shaffer's *Amadeus* in 1979, the British stage has been swept by a wave of *bio-plays*, in particular plays about famous artists, and that trend has not come to an end yet. After briefly placing this development within the wider context of contemporary British drama, I want to analyse how the artists are presented in these plays, and address the question of what may have motivated so many different contemporary British dramatists to write about (fellow-) artists.

The beginning of a new era in the development of 20th century British drama is usually identified with the first performance of John Osborne's *Look Back in Anger* on the 8th May, 1956. The original assumption that this play constitutes a revolution of British theatre had, later on, to be revised in favour of the insight that *Look Back in Anger* is a development of previously existing traditions regarding both form and content. Osborne and other dramatists of his time expressed the feelings of that generation: they were disappointed about post-war developments. On the personal level, many had benefitted from the law on education of 1944, which enabled working-class children easier access to school and university (Dietrich, 1974: 745). Although improved possibilities of education are desirable, in this case they led to a state of disorientation and to the children's alienation from their original social environment, which was not necessarily replaced by new social connections. The resultant disillusionment of the younger generation on the personal level was enhanced by political events such as the Suez crisis, the Soviet invasion of Hungary, and the beginning of the Cold War. Many of the dramatists themselves (Osborne, Wesker, Pinter) were working-class . In dramatizing the problems of their own generation, they frequently wrote about social groups that had hardly been characters in drama before: the working classes, adolescents, old and ill people. The way of presentation was often naturalistic (Tynan, 1984: 178). John Russell Taylor has thoroughly analyzed this phase, and the title of his book coined its name: *Anger and After* (1962).

The social and political events of 1968, the student unrests, the crushing of the democratization in Prague, the Vietnam war, and the cultural revolution in China were indirectly reflected in the British theatre scene. One indication is the significant increase of alternative theatres: Wolter lists sixteen new establishments in 1968, such as Portable

Theatre, Interaction, Pip Simmons Group, and Red Ladder Theatre (1980: 136). These so-called 'fringe theatres' formed a forum for the young and politically oriented dramatists, They wanted to

> integrate theatre more strongly into day-to-day life. The general tendency was to make the spectator not look up to an elevated sphere of culture, but to bring theatre literally to the people: onto the street, into the factory, into the pub, into youth hostels and local communication centres.
>
> (Enkemann, 1980: 499)

Another very important factor in this time was the abolition of censorship, which enabled more and different subject-matters to be treated on the British stage than before. Many dramatists who wrote at that time were socialist, such as David Hare, Howard Brenton, Trevor Griffiths, and Stephen Poliakoff. But traditional genres were also pursued further, by dramatists such as Stoppard, Gray, Hampton, Ayckbourn, Bond, Shaffer, Storey, or Pinter (Hayman, 1979: 68–70)

Approximately around the middle of the seventies the original verve, which had arisen at the end of the sixties, decreased considerably. Dramatists' concern shifted from general political and theoretical questions to a more individual perspective. This tendency continued throughout the eighties, with an emphasis on the following subject-matters: questions of education (e.g. Willy Russell, *Educating Rita* [1986]; Simon Gray, *Quartermain's Terms* [1983]); the situation of disabled people (e.g. Brian Clark, *Whose Life is it Anyway?* [1978]; Phil Young, *Crystal Clear* [1983]); the role of man and woman and the importance of the family (e.g. Caryl Churchill, *Top Girls* [1982]); the conflict in Northern Ireland (e.g. *Translations* [1980] and other plays by Brian Friel); the nuclear threat (e.g. Brian Clark, *The Petition* [1986]); national socialism (e.g. C. P. Taylor, *Good* [1981]), as well as plays about the problems faced by the English middle classes (e.g. Alan Ayckbourn, *Season's Greetings* [1982]). Problems of the individual are central to all those plays.

This statement holds true especially for the plays that are at the centre of this essay – those about famous historical artists. Between 1900 and 1977, about eighty such plays were written, compared to well over two 200 in the much shorter time period of 1978–2000. Those plays have in common that within their dramatic world the main character(s) is (are) from the world of history, i.e., artists who gained fame during or after their lives. The dramatists of biographical plays about artists made ample use of available historical documents, such as the artists' autobiographies, letters, biographies, and statements of various kinds from the artists' friends. Independent of the extent of the dramatist's reliance on the sources, the resulting plays may be placed on a scale of high authenticity when the dramatist tries to present a historically accurate picture of the artists concerned, and low authenticity, when a specific historical artist serves 'merely' as an inspiration for a play about an artist who is not necessarily intended as a representation of the historical inspiration. Many one-person shows about famous artists are based exclusively on a compilation of historical material, whereas Kempinski's *Duet for One*, about a violinist suffering from MS, was inspired by the similar case of cellist Jacqueline du Pré (1945–1987). In Ronald Harwood's *The Dresser*, the central artist character is Sir, of the old actor/manager tradition. Since the author was, early on in his career, dresser to one of the last actor-managers, Sir Donald Wolfit, it is assumed that the character of Sir has been created with Wolfit in mind. Harwood was at pains to emphasise, however, that

> Sir is not Wolfit. Norman's [the dresser of the title] relationship with Sir is not mine with Wolfit. Her ladyship [Sir's wife in the play] is quite unlike Rosalind Iden (Lady Wolfit).
>
> (1980: 9)

Apart from the level of authenticity presented in bio-plays, another criterion of classification is the function of the artist characters within the plays. Edna O'Brien's *Virginia* (1981) and Stephen MacDonald's *Not About Heroes* (1983) focus on the famous artists' lives directly, whereas in others, the historical artist characters serve the function to exemplify a wider issue. In Christopher Hampton's *Tales from Hollywood* (1983), for example, Bertolt Brecht and Thomas and Heinrich Mann represent, among others, the Second World War emigrants from Germany to Hollywood. Brecht tries hard to use his time in Hollywood as much as possible, seeking to change the world through theatre. Thomas Mann is able to perceive the suffering of those remaining behind in Germany, and tries to help, albeit ineffectually in his elitist-intellectual ways. The character of Heinrich Mann serves to emphasise the general feeling of loneliness of all the emigrants in a foreign country. Together, the artist characters exemplify the issues of political inefficiency and cowardice of the emigrant artists and intellectuals: 'Intellectuals do not achieve anything, politics and society steamroll over them, which is their own fault, to a large extent' (Westecker, 1983).

Dusty Hughes' *Futurists* (1986) shows the artistic-intellectual life of Russia in 1921, only a few years after the revolution. Among the play's characters are Mayakovsky, Anna Akhmatova, Osip Mandelstam, Alexander Blok, Kolia Gumilyov, Lili Brik and Maxim Gorki. Those artist characters mirror the unrest of their time. Different groupings of the artists try to develop the form or art most suitable to express the revolution, with its fundamental changes of inner and outer life. Proletcultists propagate a simple language of poetry, accessible in particular to the working classes; thus they are hostile towards the acmeists and futurists, because those appear to be too elitist and academic and thus incomprehensible to the proletariat. Futurists and acmeists, in turn, accuse the proletcultists of not being working-class themselves, and thus not having any right to speak for the workers.

Master Class (1983) by David Pownall represents middle ground between bio-plays that focus on the artists for the artist's sake, and those in which the artist characters serve a more general function. The artist characters in *Master Class*, Prokofiev and Shostakovich, demonstrate that art cannot be prescribed and purpose-made to serve an ultimately un-artistic goal. In that sense, art and artists are independent, in this case of the dictator Stalin's moods: the play is set in 1948, in a Kremlin ante-chamber. Stalin has summoned the two composers to explain to them personally (assisted by culture secretary Andrej Zhdanov) what correct and good Soviet music is like. Apart from focusing on the political implications of the (fictional) encounter of the four main characters, Pownall manages to present the composers' suffering and their abilities of maintaining their personal dignities and artistic integrities under duress.

A third criterion for differentiating among bio-plays about artists is the constellation of characters within the plays. Some plays show artists mainly among themselves, such as Mozart and Salieri in Shaffer's *Amadeus*, Prokofiev and Shostakovich in Pownall's *Master Class*, poets Owen and Sassoon in MacDonald's *Not About Heroes*, and Alice B. Toklas and Gertrude Stein in Wells' *Gertrude Stein and a Companion* (1985). Other plays present a wider picture, placing a central artist character amongst several other characters, not necessarily including other artists.

In the majority of bio-plays about artists, the central artist characters are not portrayed in an idealising, let alone idolising way. Rather, they are shown uncompromisingly as human beings with their good share of weakness, problems and difficulties. In Shaffer's *Amadeus*, the hitherto traditional image of genius Mozart is broken by the way Shaffer portrays the composer as childish and prone to drastic, scatological language. If such behaviour is likely to distance readers or spectators, then Mozart's genuine suffering as a result of Salieri's intrigues does much to create compassion with Mozart. The play shows distancing behaviour and compassion-raising suffering simultaneously with impressions of Mozart's musical genius, ironically mediated through Salieri, who comments, on looking at some of Mozart's scores: 'I was staring through the cage of those meticulous ink strokes at an absolute beauty' (Shaffer, 1984: 48–9). Salieri recognises that Mozart writes his scores without any corrections: 'What was evident was that Mozart was simply transcribing music … completely finished in his head. And finished as most music is never finished' (Shaffer, 1984: 48).

Many other contemporary British bio-plays about artists share the principle of placing their artist characters in, generally speaking, difficult situations or circumstances, which allow the authors to show the artist's human frailty. At the same time, however, the artist's artistic integrity survives. Thus, in *Master Class*, Pownall exposes his artists Prokofiev and Shostakovich to the literally life-threatening encounter with Stalin (and his henchman, Zhdanov). Prokofiev is physically frail, supports himself with a stick after having suffered a fall as a result of a stroke. He appears sensitive on the subject of his state of health. When Stalin attacks him with: 'Surely you don't think that you're going to get better? Once you've had one stroke … ', Prokofiev interrupts him (quite a daring thing to do!): 'I will deal with that myself, thank you. (Pownall, 1983). He is also sensitive and angry when his loyalty to Russia is put into question, when Zhdanov asks him what he was doing during the war, and when Zhdanov (again) accuses him of being a homosexual. He remains calm, however, when Stalin and Zhdanov smash a complete collection of the recordings of Prokofiev's work, record by record. He puts on a brave face when forced by Stalin to put the following words, composed by Stalin, to proper Soviet music:

> To him who has been struck in the liver
> By a snake, treacle is better suited

Than red candy. To him, who is dying of poison,
Antidote is everything.

(Pownall, 1983: 59)

In *Not About Heroes*, Stephen MacDonald dramatises the friendship of two artists: poets Siegfried Sassoon and Wilfred Owen. Whereas in *Amadeus*, genius Mozart was exposed to the machinations of mediocre Salieri, and in *Master Class*, the artist characters Prokofiev and Shostakovich were at the mercy of Stalin's whim, Owen and Sassoon have to face the anonymous power of the First World War. Virginia Woolf, the central artist character in Edna O'Brien's *Virginia*, is shown from the age of thirteen until her death in 1941, developing as a novelist, supported by her husband, Leonard. Her artistic powers as well as her relationship with Leonard are severely tested, though, by her mental illness, which takes the function of adverse elements already familiar from other bio-plays about artists.

There are many further examples of this principle of setting a famous artist, portrayed as a frail human being, against adverse conditions and demonstrating that the element of art manages to pull through. *Piaf* by Pam Gems, and *No Regrets* by Vanessa Drucker are both about Edith Piaf, who remains faithful to her class origins despite success and a series of incidents of bad luck. In Kempinski's *Duet for One*, violinist Stephanie Abrahams (based on Jacqueline du Pré) is suffering from MS. The play shows her recovery from the shock, and gradual coming to terms with her condition, over a series of six sessions with her psychiatrist. Sir, the actor/manager in Ronald Harwood's *The Dresser* is progressively disillusioned with his profession and future. Nevertheless, Harwood manages to give us a moving impression of a great artist, who rises to a climactic, epiphanic experience during the performance of *King Lear* which forms the frame of the play, and which will be last performance (he dies at the end of the play):

> Speaking 'Reason not the need', I was suddenly detached from myself. My thoughts flew. And I was observing from a great height. Go on, you bastard, I seemed to be saying or hearing. Go on, you've more to give, don't hold back, more, more, more. And I was watching Lear. Each word he spoke was fresh invented. I had no knowledge of what came next, what fate awaited him. The agony was in the moment of acting created. I saw an old man, and the old man was me. And I knew there was more to come. But what? Bliss, partial recovery, more pain and death. All this I knew I had yet to see. Outside myself, do you understand? Outside myself.

(Harwood, 1980: 70).

In some bio-plays about artists, the central artist's suffering dominates over and above their creative powers. Hampton's *Tales from Hollywood* falls into that category, as does Hughes' *Futurists*. In *Bloody Poetry* (1985), Howard Brenton dramatises the encounters of Byron and Shelley, the first in 1816, the last in 1822, the year of Shelley's death. The play lives on the contrast already evident in the title: idealising and revolutionary attitudes to life (poetry) clash with a far less than ideal reality of daily life (bloody).

91

Claire Clairemont tells Mary Shelley, her half-sister, before the first meeting of the two poets: 'We are privileged to make this journey, we are privileged to stand on this beach, and see George Byron and Bysshe Shelley met. It will be history' (Brenton, 1985: 14). This sounds very romantic indeed, but a little further on in the play, that idyll is shattered when Claire admits, under bitter tears, that her less than romantic affair with Byron made the meeting possible in the first place:

> In a hotel room, ten minutes from London, I lifted my skirt. For the good of English poetry? Long live poetry, yes, Mary? He has very bad teeth, George Byron, you know. His teeth are not good. And he has scar marks of boils on his body from something he caught from little boys in Turkey, he told me.
>
> (Brenton, 1985: 14–15)

Thus, Claire's idealism is shattered, and so are Mary Shelley's and Shelley's own. While Mary and Claire decide to take on the risk of emotional turmoil that might result from the meeting of the two poets, at least for Mary their elated mood changes to deep depression within minutes. Shelley's philosophy of life is well expressed in a passage like this:

> I do not care what I do to myself!
> I do not, George!
> Let's peel open our brains, find the soul itself! Let's blast ourselves with electrical force – cut ourselves open, wreck ourselves, turn our inside out. To find out what we are, what can be!
> That is what poets must do ...
>
> (Brenton, 1985: 44–5)

His real life, in contrast to this revolutionary ideal, is portrayed in the play as 'more than a haunting than a history'. In line with this statement from the author at the beginning of the published text, critic Michael Billington wrote about the play as 'a feverish, dream-like evocation of the political and sexual radicalism of Byron and Shelley' (1984). The haunting, feverish element is due mainly, to the Ghost of Harriet Westbrook, Shelley's late wife, who is on stage with Shelley from Act II onwards, visible to him and the audience (not the other characters), and who provides ironic comments on the action.

While *Bloody Poetry* manages to establish some insight into the genius of the artist characters involved, this is certainly not the case in Michael Hastings' *Tom and Viv*, about poet T. S. Eliot's first marriage to Vivienne Haigh Wood. In a series of more or less short episodes, events from the years 1915, 1921, 1927, 1932, 1935, 1937 and 1947 are dramatised, based on some unauthorised biographies, and in particular Vivienne's brother Maurice Haigh Wood whom Hastings interviewed over a period of five months prior to his death. The majority of scenes shows Tom and Viv fighting each other, or shows conflicts between Tom and/or Viv with Viv's parents. Only one scene indicates some sort of harmony between Tom and Viv, which is evidenced in one of the biographies (Ackroyd, 1984: 85). Eliot's genius as a poet is not evident anywhere in the play. Tom Wilkinson, who played Eliot in the first production of the play at the Royal Court in London, found this lack made it more difficult for him to portray the famous poet on stage:

> I found one of the most frustrating problems of the play was that he [Eliot] is one of towering geniuses of the 20th century and there is no evidence in the play to suggest that he was anything other than a curious sort of pervert.
>
> (1985)

Hastings was not allowed to quote from Eliot's poetry, as Matthew Evans from Eliot's publishers, Faber and Faber, confirmed in a letter to the *Times Literary Supplement* (1984). Nevertheless, there is a scene in the play in which Viv explains to her (little interested) father a passage from *The Waste Land*, then still under the title of *He do the police in different voices*. She reads lines 108–14, Tom reads lines 115 and 116. In the published text of the play, the lines are printed as follows:

> Under the firelight, under the brush her hair
> Spread out in fiery points
> Glowed into words, then would be savagely still.
> My nerves are bad tonight. Yes, bad. Stay with me.
> Speak to me. Why do you never speak?
> Speak.
> What are you thinking of? What thinking?
> What?
> I never know what you are thinking. Think.
> I think we are in rats' alley
> Where the dead men lost their bones.
>
> (78)

The arrangement of lines in *The Waste Land* does not correspond with that used in Hastings' play. 'Speak' and 'What?' originally belong to the end of the line above compared to where they have been placed by Hastings. Maybe this is merely an oversight of Hastings' publishers or the author himself, or an indication that Viv does not only provide a chaotic interpretation of the poem, but also distorts the meaning when reading it. No matter. If this passage could be quoted in Hastings' play despite the lack of permission, why not more, which could have helped to show Eliot's genius? Barber wrote in his review:

> ... the portrait of Eliot is shamefully inadequate, giving little impression of the supersubtle mind or the travelled sophisticate, and none whatever of the introspective torments and spiritual achievements of the greatest religious poet of the century. ... It is the old problem of presenting genius on stage.
>
> (1984)

In *Virginia*, Edna O'Brien managed quite well to portray Virginia Woolf's genius on stage. Virginia's love for Vita Sackville-West was introduced gently and poetically, and a three-page scene was enough to present a striking, but not revolting, impression of Virginia's mental imbalance. In the play, the language of the character Virginia is that of Virginia Woolf herself, taken from diaries and letters. In *Tom and Viv*, in contrast, Eliot's words are those of Hastings. If the author was not allowed to show Eliot's genius by quoting his poetry, why not use more of his linguistic characteristics? Wilkinson comments, based on his research for playing Eliot:

> Eliot was not an inarticulate person. You know, there was the problem that he spoke, I mean, maddeningly spoke, in sentences, in paragraphs, and if he was interrupted, he would stop at the interruption and then carry on.

(1985)

Instead of long, complex sentences we get an Eliot speaking in short main clauses, as in the following passage:

> We met an old tutor of mine. Bertie Russell has a flat in Bury Street. He insisted we share it with him. It's a room behind the kitchen where he stores china. It's large enough for a single cot, and there's a davenport. Sometimes I sleep in a deckchair in the hall.

(68)

Now I would like to discuss an aspect of the creative writing process: what inspires dramatists to write about fellow-artists? I will argue that the writing of plays about artists has to be located in a wider context of developments in society over the last 20 years – not restricted to theatre in particular or even the arts in general.

At first glance, one might be tempted to cite commercial reasons for the dramatists' interest in a type of play that appears to be commercially successful, at least potentially, as the success of *Amadeus* and *Piaf* had shown. In some cases, such an argument may be valid, especially when some plays about artists lack artistic merit and box office success. For example, *Cafe Puccini*, premiered in the West End in 1986, failed mainly because the production expected actors to sing Puccini arias, accompanied by four strings, piano, flute and accordion. Trained opera tenors have their problems with Calaf's aria *Nessun Dorma* from Puccini's *Turandot*. If an actor with some voice training attempts to sing this aria live on stage, it is, according to one critic, a laudable act of bravery, but 'no one should have done this to him or to us!' (Colvin, 1986: 21). The show closed after only forty-three performances. *After Aida* is another example of a commercially intended but not successful play, dealing with the last phase of Giuseppe Verdi's career. It played for twenty-eight performances. *Times* critic Irving Wardle wrote:

> There is no dramatic situation. The setting [the stalls of a theatre] is merely a playground where speakers can address us with memoirs, team up for brief scenes and rehearsals ... members retreat to the stalls to read newspapers or sit looking bored; a sight that leaves

you wondering why you should be interested in a spectacle they cannot be bothered to look at.

(Wardle, 1984)

Commercial reasons may also be given for the large number of one-person shows. Their productions cost less, and unemployed actors can tour in shows they have compiled and perhaps also directed themselves. David Pownall, author of *Master Class* and several other plays about composers, acknowledges the commercial reasons behind one-person plays, but adds: 'I love one man plays. I've written two, one for a woman and one for a man. As a writing exercise it is very exciting and good for me. You have to entertain with just one person on the stage,' (1985)

Commercial reasons, however, are not sufficient to explain the large number of plays about artists over the last twenty-two years. In several cases, dramatists have indicated the circumstances of writing about fellow-artists. A few examples follow. David Pownall had read the minutes of the composers' conference held by the communist party in 1948 in Moscow: 'Those minutes froze your blood on the one hand, but they also made you laugh. There was a kind of mixture of horror and mockery … and I immediately knew that I wanted to write a play about this' (Meyer-Dinkgräfe, 1985). The result is *Master Class*, which shows a fictional meeting between Stalin, Shostakovich and Prokofiev in the Kremlin. Pownall's intention in writing the play was to convey, if possible, the same feelings to the audience he had experienced while reading the minutes.

Howard Davies, who directed the original production of *Piaf* by Pam Gems in 1978, relates the circumstances that led Gems to writing for the theatre: when her children had grown up, she became interested in politics, especially feminism. She wanted to write a play with a woman as main character who should be able to discuss feminist issues intellectually, and therefore not be middle-class, because that would have turned the play into open polemics. Instead, Gems chose a working-class woman in Edith Piaf, and focused on 'how that woman managed, in a male world, to survive and hang on to take the mike and sing' (Meyer-Dinkgräfe, 1985).

While Tom Kempinski was working on *Duet for One*, he was suffering the first stages of agoraphobia. For him, the psychiatrist character in the play, Dr Feldman, and the artist, Stephanie, represented the life-supporting and life-threatening forces within himself, in his struggle between survival and suicide (Glaap, 1984). Stephen MacDonald wrote *Not About Heroes* as an attempt to find out how one man (Owen) can be so very deeply influenced by his friendship with another man (Sassoon) that his art and his life changed: 'Both of the characters had been flawed heroes of mine for a long time and I wanted others to love and admire them as much as I did' (McDonald, 1985).

The examples of Pownall, Gems, and Kempinski show that very personal events in the lives of the dramatists serve as inspirations to write a play about a fellow-artist. Generally speaking, the dramatists have to depend on their intuition, as Peter Shaffer puts it: 'One is not finally aware of why one idea insisted or the others dropped away … The playwright hopes that one will say: "Write me! Write me!"' (Buckley, 1975: 20). Many dramatists confirm that they had reached a stage in their artistic development at which they wanted to reflect about the nature of art and the implications of being an artist. Margaret Wolfit, who wrote and performed in her one-woman show on George Eliot, said:

> Whatever the artist's field is, there is something universal. You recognise in a writer something about yourself as an actress. One is drawn to certain people … . I had an extraordinary experience, actually. A few years ago I had done an awful lot of work on George Eliot, I felt I must kind of get away from her … . I must do something other than a writer. … I was walking on a road when the name of Taylor Hill came into my head. At that time I thought that she was involved in some way with photography. When I began to research into this person, I realised I didn't know anything about the woman at all. … I discovered that in fact she was linked in marriage to George Eliot. That was fascinating because I thought I was getting away from George Eliot and I was not getting away from her at all … . In some strange way you begin to think: 'What's going on? There's something in the ether that draws you to people'. I think one does learn a tremendous amount, you learn that we are all kind of linked in some strange way.
>
> (Meyer-Dinkgräfe, 1985)

Athol Fugard's *The Road to Mecca* is a further example for the phenomenon of self-referral, of the dramatist. The artist character in this play, Miss Helen, is mainly suffering from her creativity drying up. Fugard commented that writing this play 'coincided with a need in me that I hadn't recognised, a curiosity about the genesis, nature and consequence of creative energy, my own' (Smith, 1985). Three years later, with even more hindsight, Fugard wrote, on the occasion of a revival of the play in Berkeley, USA, that at the time of writing the play he had himself been preoccupied, as had his main character, Miss, Helen, with fears of his artistic creativity drying up: 'I've been frightened by that … and I explored it because I needed to. I am now 55 years old and one of the great terrors of my life is the thought of my creativity drying up before my time has ended.' (Berson, 1988: 35)

There are further examples that dealing with an artist character in a play entails, for the dramatist, dealing with himself or herself as an artist. Roland Rees directed the first theatre production of Howard Brenton's *Bloody Poetry*. The artist characters in that play, Shelley and Byron, according to Rees, represent two clear features of Brenton's own personality: 'He loves to talk to enthusiastic listeners, with a bottle of good wine, for hours. On the other hand, he has those qualities of Shelley, being passionate, romantic, and all that' (Meyer-Dinkgräfe, 1985). Discussing *Amadeus* and Edward Bond's *Bingo*, Berger supports the view that dealing with an artist in drama leads to self-referral for the dramatist. In Shaffer's case, Berger argues, the conflict of genius and mediocrity in *Amadeus* mirrors Shaffer's own oscillation between the Apollonian and the Dionysian (Berger, 1985: 219). Shaffer himself said:

> I just feel in myself that there is a constant debate going on between the violence of instinct on the one hand and the desire in my mind for order and restraint. Between the secular side of me, the fact that I have never actually been able to buy anything of official

religion and the inescapable fact that to me a life without a sense of the divine is perfectly meaningless.

(Cromwell, 1980)

The personal view of dramatists that they write about fellow-artists to find about more about their own existence as artists, the intentional or unintentional act of self-referral, is a phenomenon not limited to some isolated artists; rather, it is one example of a general tendency towards self-referral which can be observed in our time. This tendency can be located on several levels: postmodernism and the related concept of intertextuality, science and the ambiguous phenomenon of the New Age movement.

The concept of postmodernism is ambiguous in at least four main areas: some critics put the legitimacy of the concept in question, arguing that the are no new phenomena that might justify the introduction of a new term (Welsch, 1988: 13). The next issue is the field of the term's application. According to Welsch, the term originated in the North American literature debate, then spread to architecture and painting, sociology and philosophy, and by now there is hardly an area 'not infected by this virus' (Welsch, 1988: 9). As far as the time of origin is concerned, the debate originated in the USA in 1959, referring to phenomena of the 1950s; in 1975, when Europe had caught up with the development, the *New Yorker* wrote that postmodernism was out and there was demand for a post-postmodernism. In the same line of argument, Welsch quotes Umberto Eco's worries that before long even Homer would be considered postmodern. Finally, the contexts of postmodernism are ambiguous: the age of SDI (Strategic Defense Initiative) technology versus a green, ecological, alternative movement; a new integration of a fragmented society versus increased intentional fragmentation and pluralisation (Welsch, 1988: 9).

Welsch attempts to define a common denominator for different approaches to postmodernism:

> We can talk about postmodernism where a fundamental pluralism of languages, models, and procedures is practised, not just side by side in separate works, but in one and the same work, i.e. interferentially.

(1988: 15)

In the context of this discussion, the argumentation within postmodernism about the concept of text, which led to the concept of intertextuality, is important. Intertextuality can be regarded as a superimposed concept for methods of a more or less conscious, and to some extent concrete reference in the text to individual pre-texts, groups of pre-texts, or underlying codes and complexes of meaning. These methods are already established individually in literary criticism under such terms as source study, influence, quotation, allusion, parody, travesty, imitation, translation, and adaptation (Broich and Pfister, 1985: 15). Two extreme concepts of intertextuality with different points of departure can be discerned: the global model of post-structuralism regards every text as part of a global intertext. In contrast, structuralist and hermeneutic

97

models argue in favour of a more conscious, intended, and marked reference between a text and a pre-text or groups of pre-texts.

In the natural sciences, but also in the humanities and the social sciences, the last twenty years have been characterised to a large extent by an investigation of self-referral, self-organization and related phenomena. A brief look at systems theory, biology, physics, chemistry, mathematics, sociology and literary psychology will elucidate this claim.

Systems theory is the attempt to accept holistic thinking in a dynamic form, in the framework, and by help of the means of modern science, as a reaction to atomism, mechanism and physicalism-chemism (Heijl, 1983: 23). The biologist Humberto Maturana is well-known for his research in this field. In 1970 he first suggested a model of cognition which is based on systems theory and brain physiology.

Maturana's point of departure is a radical constructivism which assumes that any perception of an object, all experience, is not the image of reality, of objects, but *a priori* its construction by the subject. An essential new aspect in this approach is the central position of the observer. Self-referral, a process that goes on within the observer, leads to those phenomena traditionally called perception and understanding. The idea behind this is that a human being is an autopoietic system. One characteristic of such a system is its cyclic organisation, which can be understood as self-reproduction. All informations which the autopoietic system needs to maintain its circular organisation, are inherent in the circular organisation itself. For that reason an autopoietic system can be regarded as a closed system. This insight in turn leads to the conclusion that an autopoietic system is characterised by self-referral: the system itself defines what will be a partner in reaction to that system. The system itself defines the modality of the import, the transformation and the export of output.

If applied to human beings, these general characteristics of autopoietic systems mean the following: the human nervous system is, anatomically, a closed system, which functions in all the regions of the body as one organ by way of the network of nerve cells. This organ leads all the activities of the individual nerve cells to a holistic integration. If events take place in the environment of a human being, which have any kind of effect on the human nervous system, the nervous system suffers deformations with which it has to cope. Every act of perception comprises a series of such deformations. The nervous system itself determines what kind of deformation a certain event will be for the system, what kind of event the system experiences the deformation, and what attitude the system has towards the deformation. In interpersonal relations, the deformation can be defined as the way and the intensity which is effected by the partner of interaction. Because the definition of the deformation and the experiencing, the constructing of perception, are solely determined by the experiencing system, the partner of interaction has no direct influence on how they are perceived from their respective partners of interaction (Rusch, 1987).

Phenomena of self-reference are not only found in (human) biology, but also in physics and chemistry. At the beginning of the seventies, quantum field theories had their difficulties in explaining the phenomena they could observe in particle accelerators. The problem was based in the assumption that the respective basic fields (electro-magnetic, strong and weak interactions, gravity) had so many and such complex interactions with each other that it was difficult to clearly describe the relationships of those interactions. The discovery of the spontaneous symmetry breaking, which shows deeply hidden symmetries of nature on fundamental space-time scales, made it possible to unify electro-magnetic and weak interaction forces to an electroweak field. This unification is possible by regarding both fields as parts of the same mathematical symmetry group. Thus the interactions between the two become self-referring. Theories of 'grand unification' unify – according to the same principle – weak, strong and electromagnetic forces and particles. A further principle of symmetry, called supersymmetry, allows the unification of fields with opposed spin. By incorporating all other forces into gravity, a unified field theory is now expressed. Today, quantum field theorists work on the most elegant formulation of this unified field theory. All these developments took place during the last twenty years, and they are based on regarding the different basic forces more and more as self-referral phenomena of a unified field (Hagelin, 1987).

Occasionally, scientists try to transfer the insights in their disciplines of natural science to the human or social level. Thus, Hagelin asks whether the unified field as discussed in modern physics can be compared to a ground state of human consciousness (1987). Nobel laureate Ilya Prigogine transfers principles to society which he discovered in chemical dissipative structures.

Physical chemistry investigates the changes of systems in time. Two classes of systems can be differentiated: linear and non-linear. The important difference with reference to the phenomenon of self-reference shows itself in the context of the state of energy of a system. All systems strive towards equilibrium – a state of balanced energy.. If interaction of two previously separated systems of different levels of energy is made possible (A = 4, B = 2), an equilibrium of energy will result (C = 3). Linear systems are not far from a state of equilibrium. According to the laws of thermodynamics, they will produce only little entropy (disorder). Non-linear systems can be far from a state of equilibrium. They are referred to as dissipative structures, because they are constantly dissipating entropy into their environment. Within them, fluctuations arise, which are being enhanced by the system itself, autocatalytically. This is the self-referral aspect. For a short time the system reaches a higher level of energy, but ultimately the system reaches a state of greater orderliness and with a smaller level of energy than before the fluctuations arose. The self-referral (autocatalytic) enhancement of fluctuations is thus responsible for the system reaching a more favourable state of energy, which is, at the same time, a state characterised by more orderliness.

In mathematics, too, research into self-referral systems has yielded interesting results during the past twenty years. Benoit B. Mandelbrot discovered the Mandelbrot-set at the centre of complex numbers. This set is created by a self-referral process of iteration: one takes a simple formula, such as $z^2 + c$, with 'z' as a complex variable and 'c' as a constant complex number. One starts with a complex number which is substituted for 'z' in the equation. The result is then substituted for 'z' in the same equation. Using a computer this process can be repeated very often, and at the same time the result can be illustrated graphically on the computer screen. The resultant structures are characterised by a striking phenomenon: the border areas of the main structure show, if sufficiently enlarged, structures that are in themselves similar to the main structure. This is called self-similarity, and it is regarded as an expression of the process of the self-structuring of the infinite complex level of numbers – chaos transforms into order (Dewdney, 1987).

Self-referral has been taken up by other disciplines than the natural sciences. The approach of radical constructivism, for example, has influenced the social sciences with an emphasis on the importance of the sociologist (Heijl, 1983).In the humanities, empirical literary theory is an example of the same influence (Schmidt, 1980).

The tendency in the natural sciences to do research into phenomena of self-referral, attempts of scientists to transfer their findings to the human and social level, and also the attempts of scholars in the humanities and the social sciences to adapt the models of self-reference suggested by the natural sciences, and to develop their own models of self-reference are all reflected, on a more popular level, by the key role that the concept of self-organisation has in the so-called New Age movement. In the different disciplines of the sciences, the same concept of self-referral has its different forms of expression. This holds true also of the usage of the term in the New Age movement, where it refers specifically to humans.

New Age tendencies have been described as a large social movement, which is very polyvalent and complex, but which is still focused on one aim: to create a new conception of the world, which acknowledges the interdependence of all phenomena in the universe (Kollbrunner, 1987). A close analysis of this movement, which also appeared under such names as 'The Turning Point' (Capra, 1983) or 'The Aquarian Conspiracy' (Ferguson, 1981) reveals twelve concepts that are of basic importance to the New Age movement. It includes self-organisation, which is closely related to self-referral discussed in the sciences. Theories first developed to account for phenomena studied in the natural sciences have been applied to the social and individual dimensions, emphasising values such as creativity, flexibility, autonomy, self-realization, common goals, decentralisation, independence, and pluralism (Schorsch, 1988).

Self-referral constitutes a major issue of insight and debate in the late 20th century. Defining and discussing the writing of plays about artists as an act of self-referral for the dramatist concerned, enables us to view the wave of plays about artists in Britain in a broader perspective. Further research is required, addressing the specific nature of the relationship between artistic creativity and *Zeitgeist*, or assessing the question why this wave of plays about artists seems to be a predominantly British phenomenon.

8 The Professional Archaeologist and The Aesthetics of Cultural Imperialism in Tony Harrison's *The Trackers of Oxyrynchus*

Alison Forsyth

Victorian plunderers and the reconstruction of the classics

Central to an appreciation of *The Trackers of Oxyrynchus* (1988) is the archaeological impetus behind the uncovering of the source text, Sophocles' Satyr play, *Ichneutae* (1996)[1]. Not only do we subsequently engage with the source text, but also with the archaeological event that brought the text to light which is in itself intrinsically informative about our culture, and which is an historical event that potentially alters the meaning of the source text in the present. The rewriting of the fragmented Sophoclean satyr play, and the re-inscribing of the archaeological event that brought the play to our attention, enhances our understanding of events subsequent to the source text, most notably cultural imperialism. In this respect, Harrison polemicises the role played by professional archaeologists in the *construction* of British history and he not only dramaturgically echoes Alun Munslow's words that 'History, like the past, is a site under construction' (1997: 18), but also he participates in its subsequent *deconstruction*.

C. M. Hinsley has described European archaeology during the second half of the nineteenth century as being very much motivated by constructively idealised and sanitised agendas that reflected '… notions of colonial power and appropriation, technological prowess and male presentation of treasures to metropolitan females' (1989: 88). Such idealisation is addressed by Harrison, not only with respect to the chauvinistic and high flown nationalistic aims expressed by Grenfell and Hunt throughout the play, but also, for example, by way of Kyllene, a representation of the Victorians' vicarious idealisation of womanhood through classical artefacts – haughty, poised and unapproachable. Indeed, late nineteenth century British archaeology was very much directed towards and shaped by an agenda infused with Victorian morality and ideals, and was a far cry from being a serendipitous, impartial and objective approach to the past, a point elaborated by the archaeologist Shelby Brown:

Classical archaeology has been tied ... to the collecting and displaying of 'good art' and the value judgements that accompany the identification of 'art' as well as the definition of 'good' (hence the traditional focus, for example, on fine wares rather than household ceramics, and patrician or imperial rather than plebeian imagery.

(1993: 246)

A 'goal oriented'[2] (Brown, 1993: 246) archaeological production line that abets personal histories to 'victory' over the vicissitudes of historical time, is suggested in *The Trackers of Oxyrynchus* not only by the farcical 'relay race' but also the drill-like militarism exhibited by Grenfell and Hunt to reach their destination. The metaphorical 'finishing line' for both archaeologists in Harrison's play is the material physical object of the text, any text, by Sophocles. It is the relative obscurity and intratextual 'loss' of art which motivates Grenfell and Hunt to value such art, and they characterise the extent to which art has become aestheticised and prejudged according to extratextual criteria even before it has even come to light. In contradistinction to the following summation of Benjamin's 'ideal archaeologist', Grenfell and Hunt are examples of the career archaeologists of the late nineteenth century, and through Harrison's carefully rewritten version of the source text we are invited to consider the part such 'professionals' have played in the artificial and false construction of 'culture':

The true archaeologist is no treasure hunter though. For him or her, a shard of pottery, a broken comb, a worn out shoe, may have ... greater worth than the gold and silver treasures of the past ... it is the archaeologist who recognises that beneath our feet are the countless bones and remains of those who have no monument, no landmark.

(Benjamin, 1985: 314)

Harrison's play highlights the programmatic impetus behind Grenfell and Hunt's quest in order to emphasise, by virtue of historical hindsight, how futile the explorers' attempt to 'make' history really is, for, just as Gadamer points out, it is *we* who are continuously made and shaped by history:

In truth history does not belong to us, but instead we belong to it. Long before we understand ourselves reflectively, we understand ourselves in a self-evident way through the family, society and state in which we live ... .

(1989: 276)

Grenfell's concerted dismissal of the 'petitions' as being merely administrative 'non-art' is ironically revealing for today's audience, particularly when one considers that the self-same petitions have subsequently disclosed the 'selectivity' of cultural imperialism as well as throwing light on what was perceived by the Athenian hegemony to be the potentially dangerous, 'democratising' influence of Satyr drama.

'Theogenising' origins and generic over-determination

Closely bound up with Harrison's critique of programmatic and imperialistically motivated archaeology is the dramaturgical highlighting of the aestheticisation of art, an issue that is central to the source text. Grenfell and Hunt perpetuate an aestheticising project that has appropriated and consigned Satyr drama to predetermined and often divisive evaluations. In this respect, the way in which the characters/actors of Grenfell and Hunt double up as Apollo and Silenus is fitting because it forges clear links between the 'professional' Victorian cultural imperialists and the earliest aestheticisation of art, namely the Apollonian domination and rationalisation of Dionysian spirit.

Satyr drama is the earliest known dramaturgical example of a concerted institutional evaluation of art, even though for a short period it transcended such categorisation at the competitive Dionysian festivals. Indeed, Tony Harrison pinpoints these festivals as rare occasions when a 'great amalgam' of spectators from 'the shoemaker' to 'the philosopher' voted, according to their particular response on the 'effect' of art. In this respect, Harrison's Rewrite of the Sophoclean Satyr drama, is an ideal resource for his dramaturgical consideration of the aestheticisation of art, not only because of the demise of the satyric genre but with respect to the overriding thematic concern of the source text, the Apollonian rationalisation of art. Because Satyr drama was a short-lived aesthetic category its subsequent reception has been negative and it has been casually disregarded as a frivolous unstructured aberration with which the Greek tragedians completed their tetralogies. However, Harrison's play, in keeping with the hermeneutic emphasis on questioning, interrogates our complacent acceptance that the demise of the Satyr was due to its intrinsic worthlessness. Thus, through an almost Foucauldian cross-examination of the very discursive practices that shape us, Harrison assumes a critical scepticism toward the naturalised state of 'aesthetic consciousness' that dictates much of our reception of art – a process highlighted by Hernnstein Smith's following comment:

> [The] ... classics have been so thoroughly evaluated and interpreted for us by the very culture and cultural institutions through which they have been presented and by which we ourselves have been formed.
>
> (1988: 51)

Thompson convincingly suggests that Tragedy arose from the less organised parameters of cultic worship, procession and hymn which gradually came to be assimilated into a new 'sanitised' form befitting the increasingly refined and aesthetically conscious city-state festivals of Dionysia. It was only the gradual 'refinement' of the tragic form once imbued with the Dionysian frenzy of cultic worship, that led to the almost generic evolution of the satyr drama, as explained by Thompson:

> This [the absorption of the Dionysian cultic rituals into the official state festivals] created a new tension, which had an important effect on its development. While the middle class strove to refine its intellectual content and to remove it from direct contact with reality,

the peasantry and plebeians continued to seek in it the fulfilment of its earlier function. The result was that, as Aristotle says, it took a long time to become serious. Indeed, the comic element was never entirely eliminated. While it was being extruded from the tragedies, it reappeared in the satyr play and on this basis at the end of the sixth century the art-form attained a final equilibrium which owed its stability to the fact that in the meantime the comic element was finding a new and independent outlet. Thus the evolution of tragedy and the emergence of comedy were both directly related to the inter-play of internal tensions that were the dynamics of society.

(1980: 222–3)

The fading Satyr Drama not only retrospectively defined what was to become the genre of Tragedy, but it also paved the way for the emergence of Comedy. Meanwhile, the residual satyr play managed to fill an increasingly ignored and less popular bucolic space that neither conformed to nor reflected the urban and civic concerns of an increasingly sophisticated and irreligious Athenian audience. The precise details of how the Athenians responded to the Satyr Drama during this transitional period are unclear, but undoubtedly the Satyr Drama has been erroneously categorised and subsequently dismissed as a short-lived frivolity that provided a concluding element of humour to the tetralogies[3]. As Todorov astutely points out, all genres, however obscure, are intrinsic to other genres and even more so with respect to the formation of the two genres which were to provide the bedrock of our cultural heritage, Tragedy and Comedy:

A new genre is always the transformation of an earlier one or of several: by inversion, by displacement, by combination … . There has never been a literature without genres; it is a system in constant transformation and historically speaking the question of origins cannot be separated from the terrain of genres themselves.

(1980: 15)

The Satyr Drama was the generic sacrifice that assured the creation of both Tragedy and Comedy, as echoed in *The Trackers of Oxyrynchus* by the reference to the myth of Marsyas. Marsyas, the satyr who was flayed alive by Apollo for deigning to play the flute, represents not only the first 'tragedy' but also provides a mythical explanation as to why the fearful satyrs henceforward accepted to play the 'role' of the frivolous, mischievous but innocuous clowns of Comedy. In this respect, Foucault's observations about the way we often misguidedly and idealistically 'theogenise' origins is correct, because, as I have just shown, any real investigation of 'origins' invariably heightens our understanding of what Foucault identifies as 'disparity':

… historical beginnings are lowly; not in the sense of modest or discreet like the steps of a dove, but derisive and ironic, capable of undoing every infatuation.

(1991: 79)

The genre of Comedy coming after the Satyr drama also consolidated the supposed 'refinement' of theatre, most notably with respect to the gradual erosion of the free interaction accommodated between audience, chorus and stage by action and parabasis. Indeed there is evidence that by the end of the fifth century, *proedria*, that is, the front row seats designated for civic dignitaries had been instituted, marking a permanent division within and between the audience and the performers. By the time of Menander this development was to lead to the chorus degenerating into an almost subsidiary convention within the main drama. In his introduction to *Lysistrata, The Common Chorus* (1992) Harrison comments on the way such seating/performance divisions have had the result of depriving later audiences of the temporally transcendent sense of event which imbued the early ancient performances. Today, Harrison argues, we are conditioned by modern theatre into entering into a psychically and hermeneutically time-bound spectacle in which '… we know in proscenium terms that once the curtain has risen, it has to fall.' (1992: v) Indeed, an inverted allusion to these divisive dramaturgical developments is made when Harrison incorporates a level of audience participation normally associated with the circus as opposed to 'high' art staged at illustrious venues, like The Royal National Theatre, as illustrated by the following stage directions:

> (Silenus *takes a papyrus scroll and unrolls it to reveal some fragments of the Greek papyrus, in fact, the first words of the Chorus of Satyrs in their fragmentary, incomplete state. They should be legible to all. With this he begins to teach the audience to chant the fragments until there is a strong chant which is echoed by the ancient voices of 8000 ghosts at the ancient Pythian games.)*
>
> [28. Delphi Version]

The Satyr Drama's intergeneric residual and formative influence on both Tragedy and Comedy is suggested by and reflected in *The Trackers of Oxyrynchus* – a theatrical combination and conflation of a whole host of generic classifications including the tragic, the comic, the musical, the detective story and the farce. In this way the dramaturgical form of the Rewrite absorbs and thereby demolishes, albeit in a transitory way, generic categorisation, the aestheticisation of art and evaluative opinions about 'high' and 'low' art, by evoking a multitude of genres, styles and forms within its own dramaturgical parameters. Examples of this include the monumental architecture and Victorian idealisation of the classical simultaneously represented by Kyllene, the Caryatid; the 'musical' atmosphere of the synchronised Satyric 'hoofers'; the detective genre represented by the 'Holmes and Watson' of archaeology; Fauvist-like vandalism and the defacement of institutional art; music, be it melodious, atonal, divine, classical, popular and folk; and a pastiche of generic classifications including comedy, tragedy, satyr and farce.

Throughout the play Harrison dramaturgically poses questions about the foundations of our cultural heritage. This is particularly apposite when one considers that the Satyr drama in terms of both its invention and demise represents the embryonic stages of aesthetics, and by extension, the very processes through which we receive, evaluate and even produce 'art', a point eloquently made by Silenus in *The Trackers of Oxyrynchus*:

SILENUS
Those teachers of tragedy sought to exclude
The rampant half animals as offensive and rude.
But whose eyes first beheld the Promethean blaze?

The aestheticisation of art and the subsequent introduction of 'refined' and judgmental terms of reference into the discussion of art have become so institutionalised that such evaluative language has actually progressed from being descriptive to being the impetus for the production of 'art'. Thus, rather like the retailer's orders which sets the factory conveyor belt into action, a prescriptive and aestheticised notion of art of the type clearly exhibited by Grenfell, as he maniacally scours the Oxyrynchus site for what he and the scholastic academy have already evaluated as 'high art' and masterpieces, has become the norm.

In a similar vein to Plato's forewarning about the mentally binding and often mystifyingly dangerous properties of the aetheticisation of art, Harrison reinvokes Sophocles' Ichneutae to draw attention to the continuing aestheticisation of art that defines what we call 'culture'. However, Harrison is not advocating that we join in with the urban outcasts in their Fauvist-like destruction of culture at the end of his play or that we revert to something approximating the Platonic unacculturated state of the 'city of pigs' (Plato, 1987: 122) but rather that, with the Rewrite, we 're-cognise'/re-know, and thus imaginatively overcome, the institutional attempts to further aestheticise our consciousness of art. Indeed, Harrison ingeniously manages to involve his audience in the imaginative leap out of aesthetic consciousness by actually involving them in the 'play' of his play. The methods he uses include audience participation, chanting, dissolving the dramaturgical boundaries between actors and audience, as well as re-scripting each version of his play for a specific and particular setting. For example, The Royal National Theatre version's enforced audience participation makes it less easy for the audience to dissociate themselves from the reality of the 'satyr' strewn walk-ways of the South Bank, outside the theatre, through either a process of aesthetic distancing or by the even more dangerous propensity to aestheticize life.

Harrison does not just arouse the audience's consciousness of the part played by aestheticisation in the formation of what we know to be 'culture' but he compels us to confront the wider social implications of continuing to adhere to an aesthetic myth which in effect serves as an inhumane and impervious shield against not only the real tragedies which abound in modern society, but also to question the imaginative and productive exertion of our hermeneutic faculties.. Indeed, the relative ignorance with which we receive the Satyr drama is alluded to in *The Trackers of Oxyrynchus* when the audience is invited to blindly 'read' and recite the projected ancient Greek text. In this way, Harrison dramaturgically emphasises how aesthetic distancing leads most of us to complacently accept and rely on the scholastic evaluations made by 'experts' like Grenfell, a far cry from the celebratory and festive amalgam cited by Harrison, and further evidence of that which Nietzsche identified as art's loss of 'effect'[4]. Thus, a generic 'knowledge' of the Satyr play has overwhelmed textual 'understanding' and as such the Satyr play is invariably but erroneously categorised as being the final 'light relief' of the tetralogies. This is indicative of the often sedimented, predetermined and elitist approach with which we receive art, as characterised by Kyllene when she states:

> (*Enter* KYLLENE *through papyrus curtain*)
> (*Looking down from stage*)
>
> I have a feeling I'm in the wrong show!
>
> [Delphi Version, 37]

Archaeological indictment and contrapuntal re-scripting

Trackers not only draws attention to the often unnoticed aestheticisation of art, of which the Satyr drama was apparently the first institutionalised victim, but also, by dint of the very site-specific nature of archaeology, it initiates a consideration of the spatiality of history, and the effects of, for example, cultural diaspora and imperialism upon our reception of art. The potential cultural dislocation suggested by the archaeological is frequently and victoriously alluded to by the colonial plunderers, Grenfell and Hunt, and in this way the archaeological event summons up not only the 'then' and 'now' of chronological time, but also the 'there' and 'here' of cultural imperialism.

> **GRENFELL**
> Here are treasures crated, waiting to be shipped
> From Egypt to Oxford where we work out each script.
>
> [Delphi Version, 9]

In this way Harrison's rescripted Rewrite refuses the audience the luxury of consigning the less comfortable and ignoble aspects of our culture to the 'past'. The very materiality and physical presence summoned up by the archaeological event, tangibly transporting the 'then' to the 'now' and the 'there' to the 'here', emphasises the continuing effects in the present of a dark and murky, but frequently and constructively 'forgotten' (Nietzsche, 1994: 62–3) past, in keeping with Said's observation:

> To a very great degree the era of high nineteenth century imperialism is over: France and Britain gave up their most splendid possessions after World War Two, and lesser powers divested themselves of their far-flung dominions. Yet once again recalling the words of T. S. Eliot, although that era clearly had an identity all its own, the meaning of the imperial past is not totally contained within it, but has entered the reality of hundreds of millions of people, where its existence as shared memory and as a highly conflictual texture of culture, ideology and policy still exercises tremendous force … we must try to grasp the hegemony of the imperial ideology, which by the end of the nineteenth century had become completely embedded in the affairs of cultures whose less regrettably features we still celebrate.
>
> (1993: 11–12)

Although the two re-scripts of Harrison's Rewrite can be 'understood' individually, they can, and arguably should be approached as a composite whole comprising the juxtaposing versions of the simultaneous effects of the aestheticisation of art on either the culture of the 'empire builders' or the appropriated culture of the plundered. Harrison dramaturgically implements what Edward Said identified as a 'contrapuntal'[5] (1993: 11) approach to culture and history, which resists the impetus to follow the dominant and thus most frequently disseminated narrativisation of culture. To avoid a process akin to that which Bhabha identifies as 'narrating the nation' (Bhabha, 1990: 1) whereby the imperial powers appropriate other cultures to such an extent that they actually naturalise their plunder as *their* 'national' heritage Harrison heeds the cultural dislocation intrinsic to the archaeological event:

> What an Algerian intellectual today remembers of his country's colonial past focuses severely on such events as France's military attacks on villages and the torture of prisoners during the war of liberation, on the exultation over independence in 1962; for his French counterpart, who may have taken part in Algerian affairs or whose family lived in Algeria, there is a chagrin at having 'lost' Algeria, with its schools, nicely planned cities, pleasant life – and perhaps even a sense that 'troublemakers' and communists disturbed the idyllic relationship between 'us' and 'them'.
>
> (Said, 1993: 11)

In the Delphi version, Harrison dramaturgically alludes to the continuing effects of the earliest stages of the aestheticisation of art into the present day, by presenting the dispossessed 'satyrs' of the present day, who, no longer acquiescing to play the role of comic clown, retaliate against their cultural alienation by making a futile and self-immolatory gesture that repeats the demise of their ancient precursors:

SILENUS
Don't burn the papyrus. That's where we come from!
(They watch the papyrus burn and drink beer and scatter the cans on the mounds where the papyri were extracted from. These are the new rubbish mounds of Oxyrynchus)

[Delphi Version, 68]

Conversely, just as the satyrs in the Royal National Theatre version are driven to destroy the very edifice of the 'culture' from which they are excluded in order to secure material insulation against the biting cold, so too, the 'cultivated' theatre audience simultaneously attempt to psychologically insulate themselves from any external suffering which might impinge upon what they perceive to be their inviolable sense of 'culture'.

The archaeological event that prompts Harrison's consideration of Sophocles' Satyr play summons up the intratextual void of survival between the textual source and its destination, simultaneously representing the latest and earliest stage of culture as we have come to know it. In addition, the archaeological event raises issues about evaluation of art into 'high' and 'low', because the first victim of negative aesthetic evaluation, the Satyr drama, is transformed in the present purely by virtue of its antiquity, authorial oeuvre and survival. Despite having been lost for thousands of years, antiquity and endurance combine to make Sophocles' fragments 'high art' in the eyes of Grenfell and Hunt, and the raw material for sell-out runs at the Royal National Theatre – a phenomenon that Foucault observes in his consideration of the aesthetic bestowal of classic status: '... their ancientness, whether real or imagined, was regarded as a sufficient guarantee of their status' (Foucault, 1991: 109). Ironically, the archaeological event which uncovered *Trackers* provides a focus for a debate about the 'value' of loss and the way authorial oeuvre, antiquity and survival can bestow kudos on play-texts that will probably never be performed, albeit in a rewritten form penned by a rather modish and currently acclaimed dramatist.

A historiography founded on 'effective history' is far removed from that displayed by Grenfell and Hunt who personify an overwhelming historicism similar to that which Nietzsche identified as 'monumental' and 'antiquarian' (1994: 62–3) uses of history. In keeping with the arrogance of their cultural imperialism and colonial spirit, these scholastic empire-builders neither question their motives, nor do they reflect on the havoc and destruction they wreak throughout the lands they pillage, for what is, in effect, cultural booty. The two versions of *Trackers* convey the antithetical results of cultural appropriation, be it the elevated aestheticisation of the classics at the bourgeois theatre, or the pillaged and appropriated who self-consciously embrace cultural abandonment in favour of the immediacy and competitiveness of sporting entertainment. In this way, Harrison takes a genealogical approach to the classic, which emphasises the contradictory and overlapping arbitrariness of interpretation and evaluation whereby '... universals of our humanism are revealed as the result of the contingent emergence of imposed interpretation.' (Foucault, 1991: 109) By highlighting the interpretative and evaluative discontinuities, contradictions and fluctuations of art, Harrison's Rewrite also draws attention to his own interpretative contingency, ephemerality and finitude, '... and that he himself is produced by what he is studying, and consequently he can never stand outside it.' (Foucault, 1991: 109) This interpretative finitude is further emphasised by Harrison's self-referential observation that in an age of accelerated gratification, aestheticisation of art is transforming into the commodification of the aesthetic and that, as a consequence, his own plays including *The Trackers of Oxyrynchus* will soon join the 'rubbish heaps' outside the theatre.

Thus, Harrison's play negotiates with history from its own acknowledged, limited and finite position and as 'the classic' represents our shared cultural practices, whether endorsed or critiqued, we are provided with a traditional and literary common ground from which to proceed, to 'understand' and to act. Just as recognition of hermeneutic finitude does not entail abdication from the hermeneutic quest to interrogate received knowledge, as prompted by a self-consciousness of one's inescapable prejudices, equally one's interpretative stance should avoid straying into the historicist's pitfall of replacing one homogenised suprahistorical interpretation with another. Indeed, the impossibility of escaping one's contingent and irreconcilably limited 'understanding' and interpretative stance is emphasised by the anachronistically confused presentation of Grenfell and Hunt's exploration, which at first appears to have taken place in 1888, only to be transposed to 1988 in Grenfell's eulogy for his archaeological mentor, Flinders Petrie:

GRENFELL
Flinders Petrie's finds were the inspiration
That puts us on the track of this present excavation.
(A hundred years ago exactly.
The date was July 1888)

[Delphi Version, 10]

Such anachronistic details alongside a pastiche of styles – artistic, linguistic and otherwise – suggest just how enmeshed and implicated we are in our history and the deeds of our forefathers, including the inescapable legacy bequeathed by cultural imperialism to our reception and production of art in the present. To emphasise the pervasiveness of these effects Harrison not only implicitly parodies The Royal National Theatre audience's 'interest' in the classics, but even his own inextricable connection in the aestheticisation of art:

(… *The* SATYRS *move forward, shuffling towards the rubbish heaps, saying the petition in Greek and picking over the newspapers, the torn text of* The Trackers of Oxyrynchus, *National Theatre posters for* Trackers, *etc …*)

However, this is not to suggest that *The Trackers of Oxyrynchus* is a vehicle solely for dramaturgical parody, for this would be to operate, albeit oppositionally, within the same discursive parameters of the aesthetics of hermeneutics which Harrison critiques. Rather, Harrison illustrates through his extremely self-conscious use of parody, just how self-perpetuating the aestheticisation of art is, particularly if we allow ourselves to become distanced from perceiving the classics as text in the present and as hermeneutic resources for 'understanding' today, as opposed to epistemological objects *of* knowledge. Harrison simultaneously uses *and* critiques parody as being intrinsically bound up with, and thus instrumental in, the perpetuation of the aestheticisation of art, with for example the presentation of Kyllene, the Caryatid. At one level Kyllene is a corrupt, although somewhat naïve and unsubtle idealisation of antiquity which arouses laughter but which, on another level, creates an uncomfortable awareness of our own, although different, self conscious aestheticisation of art. Harrison reminds us that just as the Victorians aestheticised and thus elevated what was, in effect, culturally appropriated plunder, we too, are complicit in a similar aestheticisation of life when using an inappropriately romanticised register like 'pale boy' when referring to the down and outs on the streets of London. In this respect, Harrison comments upon the way in which art has been corrupted into an aesthetic tool in the service of the 'will to power', whether that be motivated by imperialism, elitism or class division.

The legacy of loss

As opposed to being an exercise in a melancholic recuperation of a lost Dionysian spirit akin to Nietzsche's selective and 'critical' historiography6 (1994: 62–3), Harrison critiques a retrospective and highly selective re-construction of 'culture' that, as illustrated by

Grenfell and Hunt is all too often motivated by nationalism and imperialism. As his name implies 'Hunt' personifies the fearless and unsentimental acquisitiveness of the archetypal nineteenth century empire-builder with a self-proclaimed mission to import 'culture' into England's 'green and pleasant land' at the expense of what he considers to be the 'compost' and 'fertilizer' for a geographical and a cultural wasteland. Grenfell and Hunt's 'civilising' mission in the face of the fellaheen's material poverty and hunger is one that deprives and withdraws an 'organic' sense of tradition and cultural 'sustenance' from a nation. However, as Harrison's use of confusing dates and periodisation implies, Grenfell exists not only in the past but also in the present, the tortured embodiment of the recurring psychological 'myth' of a fallen but benevolent, fertile and civilising mission that was England's 'Old Empire'. Just as it is the melancholic's disposition to repeat traumatic events in an attempt to disavow them, Grenfell's frenzied determination to find and thus repeat Apollonian domination, (a mythic metaphor not only for the aestheticisation of art but, by extension, the aestheticisation of plunder for the purposes of the imperial mission) is an attempt to recuperate his sense of 'professional' purpose. Indeed, one can consider the depiction of Grenfell's physical 'possession' by the Apollonian spirit of dominion as being not only indicative of the self-generative power of aestheticisation but also expressive of the extent to which he has been overtaken by such a disavowal by repetition:

> ... the melancholic remains caught in the compulsion to repeat the trauma of loss in order to master it (a thing that he has never properly done).
>
> (Wheeler, 1995: 81)

Grenfell, like the melancholic who remains caught in the compulsion to repeat the trauma of loss, exhibits what Santner identifies as the elegiac loop of disavowal. This is emphasised by his elegiac reminiscences about Flinders Petrie and his early career that anachronistically appear to have reached the date of the performance of Harrison's play, 1988. In this respect, Grenfell's melancholia symbolises the oft-repeated and constructed histories of imperialism, or that which Santner calls fetish narratives. According to Santner, such a retroactively constructed fetish narrative:

> ... is the way an inability or refusal to mourn emplots traumatic events; it is a strategy of undoing, in fantasy, the need for mourning by stimulating a condition of intactness, typically by situating the site and origin of loss elsewhere. Narrative fetishism releases one from the burden of having to reconstitute one's self-identity under the 'post-traumatic' conditions: in narrative fetishism, the 'post' is indefinitely postponed.
>
> (Santner, 1992: 144)

Similarly, the satyr's football match as depicted in the Delphi Version of the play might well be considered a sporting repetition or 'playing out' of the cultural loss suffered as a result of what Harrison calls 'the struggle for art' with Apollonian/Imperial might. Thus, the transitory excitement of the game provides the disaffected satyrs with some kind of melancholic recuperative compensation for their demise whilst materially bearing witness to it:

> (*Enter the new generation of* SATYRS. *They are like football hooligans with scarves, flags, etc, and chanting and clapping. The* SATYRS *spray the name Marsyas ... first with red, then with white aerosol paints, the colours of the Greek team Olympiakos. They add Marsyas in blue for England.* (*Marsyas! Marsyas! Marsyas!*)

[Delphi Version, 67]

At the end of the Delphi version of the play, Harrison presents the satyrs as participants in the spontaneous and immediate gratification of competitive sport, devoid of any conscious sense of tradition (save for the ironic references made to Marsyas during the course of their repetitive and mindless chanting). The irreverent context in which the satyrs make reference to Marsyas is indicative perhaps of how far removed and desensitised they have become from their cultural roots, although subconsciously they melancholically reinvoke the initial scene of their demise. As a consequence of the imperialistic plundering and appropriation perpetrated by colonial adventurers like Grenfell and Hunt, the Delphi satyrs have reacted against and 'hijacked' a culture from which they are excluded, and they contemptuously disassociate themselves from Silenus and the older generation who accede to playing the demeaning role of 'Uncle Tom'. In addition, vernacular and colloquial terms like 'hijacked' not only serve to contemporise the demise of the satyrs, but also they draw attention to the effects of imperialism, such as the emergence of multifarious terrorist groups as a direct result of the 'daylight robbery' perpetrated by men like Grenfell and Hunt, a century earlier.

Conversely, the accusatory and violent ending of The Royal National Theatre version of Harrison's play is directed at an audience which has been shaped and is thus implicated in an imperialistic heritage which has not only continued to aestheticise art, but which has aestheticised art for imperialistic and nationalistic reasons. The incrementally binding effect of aestheticisation, as highlighted by Harrison's re-script for The Royal National Theatre, not only emphasises the fact that 'civilisation' has been founded on a myth that obfuscates any real understanding of art, but it also stresses the way in which an aestheticisation process has evolved in a 'civilisation' which inoculates itself from the omnipresent barbarity lurking beneath the institutional honours, medals and accolades of empire building – the very laurels of victory which are ironically dismissed by the Satyrs when they barter with Apollo for *their* reward:

> Summat solid, Lord Apollo, please
> Not leaf equivalents of OBEs.

[Delphi Version 26]

The Trackers of Oxyrynchus not only reinvokes the Satyr drama and its subsequent demise to polemicise our inextricable implication in the aestheticisation of art, but it also implies that such aestheticisation has gradually assumed societal proportions whereby we not only endorse cultural division, but actually assume an inoculating cynicism which allows us to aestheticise the injustice, horror and ugliness that stalks our divided society. Indeed, a disconcerting confusion is created amongst the audience when Harrison forces them to reassess their value-system by implicitly posing the following questions: do they embrace the retaliatory gesture of the 'fellaheen' and 'down and outs' against the symbolic power that suppresses them, namely their use of fragments and papyri for sorely needed fuel? *Or* are their 'aesthetic' sensibilities, as an audience, so affronted that their concerns rest with the deprivation their 'civilisation' will incur as a result of this act of cultural hooliganism and philistinism?

Although both versions of the play ostensibly and syllogistically suggest that Grenfall/Apollo is victorious in his quest to suppress the Satyr play, the material and textual reality of the Rewrite of Sophocles' *Ichneutae* can be viewed as Harrison dramaturgically throwing down the gauntlet to a potential audience. Harrison challenges the audience to contest the hermeneutic distortion of the Satyr play, be that in the form of aestheticised plunder behind a showcase in the Bodleian, or by way of a second satyr being mercilessly flayed by the returning and avenging Apollo in the name of the further rationalisation and aestheticisation of art.

The polysemic re-scripts of the Rewrite thus represent what Gadamer would refer to as 'thoughtful mediation with contemporary life' (1989: 169) because they reflect the different and distinctive historical 'effect' of the play at The Royal National Theatre to the 'effect' at Delphi; a dramaturgical recognition of the plundering legacy of professional archaeology with its impetus to requisition and transport cultural booty from one part of the world to another. In this way Harrison not only counters the criticism that he is committing the very crime of aesthetic homogenisation that he critiques, but also he displays the historically effected consciousness that typically motivates the Rewrite. Thus, Harrison's 'rewrites' of the Rewrite display a certain sensitivity to the locus of the staging of the plays, which facilitates a further emphasis and refinement of his historiographical critique of the aestheticisation of art, particularly relating to the effects of imperialism. In this respect Harrison takes full account of imperialism and its inevitable impact on the process of the aestheticisation of art that, during the nineteenth century, became even more complex in view of its association with cultural appropriation for nationalistic purposes.

Harrison prompts us to consider the psychological dimensions, including the 'will to power' behind culture and its continuing construction, not least by virtue of the very fact that we are imaginatively transposed into a world of satyrs and gods through the psyches of the two men, Grenfell and Hunt. The 'humanity' of the myth is dramaturgically emphasised by the simultaneous casting of the actors who play Grenfell and Hunt as the mythical Apollo and Silenus respectively. The dramaturgical humanisation of what is, in accordance with 'aesthetic' practice, designated a myth, prevents us, the cultural heirs to Grenfell and Hunt's legacy, from securing a fictional or mythical bolt-hole to which we might escape from our hermeneutic responsibilities. In this way the Apollonian cruelty toward Marsyas and the subsequent demise of the Satyr Drama wrought by the aestheticisation of art is very clearly portrayed as being pertinent to and connected with our present realities. By 'humanising' the Apollonian spirit of dominion Harrison convincingly forges a connection between such mythical brutality and the self-same process which was to become intrinsic to the cultural imperialism of the nineteenth century and upon which so much of the subsequent 'culture' as we know it is founded and sustained today.

Notes

1. Sophocles' *Ichneutae is* based on a Homeric hymn to Hermes, and concerns the pilfering of Apollo's cattle whereby Hermes, the offspring of Maia and Zeus, led the herd in such a way so as to reverse and confuse their tracks and thus conceal their own footprints, in an attempt to elude apprehension by the angry Apollo. Only fragments of the *Ichneutae* survive, about half the original text. See the Loeb Classical Library, Sophocles III (ed.) G. P. Goold *Sophocles' Fragments: The Searchers* trans. by Hugh Lloyd-Jones, LCL 483, Cambridge, Mass: Harvard University Press, 1996, pp. 140–177.

2. Brown refers to the useful distinction made by Sabloff with respect to the uses and implementation of archaeology – namely between the 'dynamic' and the 'static' past, the former of which, unlike Grenfell and Hunt's practices, takes a processual and postprocessual approach to archaeology. See Sabloff, Jeremy 'When the Rhetoric Fades: A Brief Appraisal of Intellectual Trends in American Archaeology During the Past Two Decades' in *Bulletin of the American Schools of Oriental Research* 242: 1–6 1981/3

3. The earliest recorded attribution of a Satyr play is to Pratinas of Phleious, who later competed with Aeschylus between 499 and 496 BC. Evidence shows that Pratinas wrote fifty plays of which thirty two were satyric, implying that he must have been competing at Athens before the rule of tetralogy came into force in 502–1 BC. Such empirical facts suggest that the genre of Satyr drama was probably far more popular than the textual evidence would suggest, but that further investigation is circumscribed to a large degree because the Satyr drama flourished before its retrospective categorisation as the first dramaturgical 'creation', and its subsequent demise, soon after, as the first victim of the aestheticisation of art. However, it should be observed that Satyr drama did not disappear completely and suddenly; in fact there is evidence to suggest that it was still relatively popular up until the third century and Seaford argues this clearly proves that the ancient rituals, soil and nature which unite the mythological satyrs were nostalgically lauded by the Athenians during a period of rapid urbanisation. [See R. Seaford in the Introduction to Euripides' *Cyclops*, Oxford: Clarendon Press, 1984, p. 31.]

4. In *The Birth of Tragedy: Out of the Spirit of Music* trans. by Shaun Whiteside, London: Penguin, 1993, Nietzsche polemicises the suppression of what he calls the 'Dionysiac' spirit of encroaching rationalism and the Socratic aesthetic, which pinpoints to the work of Euripides. The true spirit of tragedy, for Nietzsche was captured in the healthy antagonism between the Dionysiac and Apollonian aspects of life, but with the demise of the Dionysian spirit as personified by satyrs, tragedy degenerated into a theoretical representation of rational optimism and poetic justice.

5. Said popularised the term 'contrapuntal' which in musical parlance quite literally means 'the art of combining melodies' [Chambers]. Here, Said attempts to combat the mono-dimensional and often overwhelmingly Eurocentric approach, or what Bernal has labelled 'continental chauvinism', to cultural studies that have prevailed by advocating a simultaneous and multi-perspectival focus to the study of cultures.

6. Here Nietzsche puts forward his ideas about critical historiography whereby he advocates the selective forgetting of history: '… one's being just as able to forget at the right time as to remember at the right time; on the possession of a powerful instinct for sensing when it is necessary to feel historically and when unhistorically. This precisely, is the proposition the reader is invited to meditate upon: the unhistorical and the historical are necessary in equal measure for the health of the individual, of a people and of a culture.'

9 Wittgenstein and Morality – The Playwright's Purpose

Dic Edwards

I want to say that I'm speaking today more as a playwright – a qualification behind which I can defend myself – than as an academic. Not only that, but, using the terminology invoked in Daniel Meyer-Dinkgräfe's original call for papers, as a working-class playwright. I'm aware, of course, of how this may seem paradoxical. I'm also argumentative and consequently much of what I say you may well feel inclined to argue with.

I would like to take you on a kind of journey from where I began as a writer, through what often seems like the war zone of where I work – in the theatre, to the play *Wittgenstein's Daughter.*

Something about the class terminology: We're talking about the professions but for the sake of my arguments that relate to class I'll be referring to the professions as the middle classes. These terms, of course, can mean different things to different people. When I use them I want you to think of the middle classes *as those in* authority and the working class *as those subject to that authority.*

I begin as a writer in the belief that the theatre means something and that it has a relevance. I think this because I believe that the professions which order our society – by making its laws, educating its children, and so on – have a moral responsibility to that society, and that theatre, which is also a profession, has an even deeper moral responsibility. This is to keep an eye on the professions on behalf of the rest of society – which I would describe as *monitoring democracy.* Theatre, therefore, needs to be relevant. I can't imagine moral activity that's irrelevant! Any failure must be serious. Unfortunately, the way I see it, it is failing.

In a recent edition of University Challenge the bonus sections of two questions, that is six questions in all, on Contemporary British Theatre failed to elicit a single correct answer. Interestingly, the answer that was given for who wrote *The Romans In Britain,* was Trevor Hall! I say interestingly because Trevor is the Christian name of one of our most prominent theatre directors and Hall is the surname of one other. Neither, of course, is a writer. On this showing, Contemporary British Theatre (in which the director looms large) would appear to have become irrelevant to even our young intellectuals. If it's not relevant to them then we're clearly in trouble. And when I say 'we' I mean all of us. Society.

I have long suspected what the University Challenge example seemed to reinforce. Certainly during the time when I was writing *Wittgenstein's Daughter*. But it is only one example. There are many more.

There is, in my opinion, what I call a *moral silence* at the heart of contemporary British Theatre.

Because of the views I have about theatre's function, I cannot separate what plays are about from the process of making them. For example, in my play *Wittgenstein's Daughter,* Alma searches for a language to give to her soon-to-be-born child. At the same time, the play itself is a search for language. It argues that there is a silence at the heart of things – a silence which I will come to talk about – invoked by Wittgenstein. A moral silence. Thus the play itself and its problems, mirrors the problems of theatre. And because these problems come out of its relationship with society, then the play is not merely abstract but a commentary on the moral silences which exist in society. The action of the play is the acting out of the consequences of applying my arguments to the problems. As we shall see, Wittgenstein himself, the professional philosopher, in my account epitomises the malevolent professional. The play debates the consequences of the moral silence.

To begin with I want to talk about why I think things are not right. Then I want to say something about where I'm coming from as a writer and what Theatre means to me before looking more closely at *Wittgenstein's Daughter.*

The most obvious manifestation of the problem – the moral silence – is that today's theatre is a predominantly middle-class pursuit. And not only that but there appears to be an almost exclusive middle-class theatre going audience. We're not getting through to even our young intellectuals because of this failure to be all embracing. And as it is almost exclusively middle-class, what about the relationship of the working class with Theatre? Let me tell you what I think this is like.

Recently, a housepainter who lives across the road from me, told me how he'd had to put his dog down. The dog was fifteen years old. There had been a deep bond between them. But, at the vet's, things had gone wrong. The vet hadn't been able to find the appropriate vein in the dog and had had to keep stabbing away at the poor animal. The last thing the housepainter heard before being overcome and leaving was his old dog crying. Crying because of the vet. The housepainter told me that he'd wanted to kill the vet. Instead, he left. He left feeling hopeless, useless, as if he'd failed the dog. For all he knew, the vet may have been drunk. No apology, but more importantly, no explanation had been given. The event was a kind of theatre. The relationship of the housepainter to this event mirrored the relationship of the working class with our theatre. How? The housepainter had left the vet's in *silence.* It's not so much that the working class leaves the theatre in silence, they don't even enter in the first place! The professional had imposed the silence. Our Contemporary Theatre imposes a silence on the working class.

The housepainter knew instinctively that there would be nothing he could say to the vet to get the understanding of the event that he needed. *They speak different languages.* These different languages are the languages of different classes. The language of the vet's world is the language of professional authority. Supposing the housepainter had asked what went wrong. The vet would have dismissed the housepainter's question in terms that would freeze him out, as though in the vet's world there is a different, specialised language that the housepainter has no right of access to. Had the working-class housepainter approached the world of the professional with questioning at an *intellectual* level, he would have got a very indignant: 'How dare you!' and been dismissed.

Silences in theatre are very important. Silences *caused* by Theatre are a very different thing!

Wittgenstein argued in his first work, the *Tractatus Logico Philisophicus*, that it's in the silences that the important things happen. The working class in its relationship with society has experience of a certain silence. I have experienced it myself. But while it may have been for me in the silence that I developed my intellect, in the silence that I have shouted about the injustices in my society and in the silences that I plot, if Wittgenstein was right when he said that it's morality that we cannot speak of in the famous last line: 'Whereof one cannot speak one must remain silent', then there may be severe implications for the working class who may seek to find some authority in the natural justice of moral codes.

If I can extend the metaphor of my story at the risk of suggesting the absurd, one might argue that a central question for our theatre could be: doesn't the housepainter deserve an explanation for what the vet did with his dog. There is, perhaps, an intellectual dimension.: How much did the dog suffer because of the low social status of its owner? Perhaps the best the housepainter could have hoped for from the vet would have been a kind of obituary for the dog. Which is what, incidentally, most of our plays about the working class are like: obituaries written by middle-class writers. No analysis of things, just description. What I call chocolate-box theatre, by which I mean, mere representational theatre. I'll come back to this. In the end, all the working-class writer is left with, perhaps, is the housepainter's desire to kill the vet – which, maybe would make a good episode for *The Bill* – but not for me. As a working-class writer, the purpose of my theatre is to bring language to the silence.

I have made this discovery: while it appears that our mainstream Theatre is for the middle class this is, in fact, an irony. It's an irony because the great truth is that Theatre is most importantly for the working class. And this is because the working class stand to gain more, ultimately from the proper functioning of the Theatre. That's not to say that there isn't a kind of theatrical activity enjoyed by the middle class which is valid. There is. And it's important. It's important because as long as it's there it reminds us of why we desperately need its alternative: what I call *analytical theatre.* Unfortunately, this analytical theatre has become a victim of the moral silence. In fact, the moral silence, you may say is the absence of analytical theatre.

The moral silence at the heart of Contemporary British Theatre is deeply pernicious. It feeds on the confusion it breeds. Perhaps most widespread is the confusion about what theatre actually is. Increasingly it seems that even people who work in the theatre are confusing it with the cinema. As though they're the same thing! A theatre play often appears to be a trial run for a screen play. And it's alarming how many stage plays often by our leading writers are translated into film with such ease and become successful. The latest best example is, I suppose, Godber's *Up and Under*.

In order to understand what Theatre is, it's important to understand what it isn't. It isn't cinema. But the moral silence in the Theatre has made people less vigilant and the distinctions are blurred. This is critical. It's critical because – as I'll show – while the relationship between the audience and the stage in a piece of real theatre is active, even creative, the relationship between the cinema audience and the screen is passive. This suggests to me that some of our most applauded plays are not really plays at all! Let me say something about this.

It's easy to be confused. Until I was about twenty, apart from the annual visit to the pantomime, the only time I sat in an audience was in the cinema. I would imagine that the pantomime would have seemed strange to a young person used to going to the cinema. The proscenium arch of the pantomime theatre was not much different from a screen. But that's as far as it went. Though there was some kind of story, which was in the end all a bit silly, it was more like the circus. Only in the circus the things that went on went on in the middle of all of you, the audience. Here, at the pantomime, people were lined up in front of you, high up, shouting. Shouting at you. In a way, cut off from you. Not like the circus. So what was it for? Other than to let you shout back and maybe throw things.

The first play I can recall seeing, was when I went with the school to a production of *Macbeth*. This was like the pantomime *and* the cinema. You all sat in this big room and you watched things take place on a stage which, from where you sat, looked like a screen – only down there there were real people running about. Not as good as cinema because they looked too small; you couldn't see their faces. More like pantomime because the people were falling over; falling over each other and falling into the bits at the back that make it look real – the scenery – and making that fall over! Difficult to work out what it was for. What was its point? Cinema does it much better. And so, as I've said, until I was about twenty I stuck to the cinema entirely.

Then, as I became political, I became aware of playwrights like Brecht and Bond. One thing I'd noticed about cinema was that it wasn't very political. It showed pictures of things but it didn't show what was going on on the inside of events. Politically. I became interested in theatre because of this political dimension. It seemed to be a place where you could discuss the problems in society at a public level; something otherwise denied, in effect, to those outside the political profession. I recalled how, at school, we'd read a play called *Strife* and I remembered I'd quite liked it. It interested me because of what it was about. It was about workers striking. But in the end, I know I'd felt disappointed. It was more like a picture; it was a description of things. Cinema can do this better. Plays must be about discussing *why*. I knew this instinctively. But *why* must theatre be about discussing why? If it was entertaining, *cinema* would be about discussing why. And even Brecht said that theatre must be entertaining. I came to feel, in desperation, that if the business of theatre and cinema was the same then why bother with theatre at all when cinema can do it much better? My conclusion was that they must be different. As social activities they'd seemed so much alike and yet I knew that the only way I was going to come to believe in theatre and want to write for it was to discover what made them different.

One day, as an adult, I took my small daughter to the circus and there I found the key to what I was looking for. The circus was a small one. Some of the acts seemed quite amateur. It even seemed in some ways, run down. The moment of this revelation which had been building as the clowns had come to us and we'd seen behind their masks and into their eyes, was watching a young woman who seemed to be not much older than my own daughter, falling from a trapeze, falling through the air *looking,* it seemed, for the trapeze that she needed to grab to stop herself from falling to the circus floor. She seemed unhappy. I realised that she and I were in the same place precisely. Inhabiting the same space. A space which included my daughter and everyone else there. My feeling of involvement with this young woman looking, *searching* for her trapeze had been total and had extended to what was happening everywhere in that tent. And because of that it seemed as if she was looking for more than just the trapeze.

It was as if we were all separate from the world in a different special world as if something was happening to us that we, collectively, needed to understand. I know you may say that this is all rubbish – I just fell in love with the girl. But even if there was something of that, it wouldn't matter. I had connected with something deeper than the sheer spectacle. And it didn't matter if it was on an emotional level. This, after all, is how Mother Courage appeals to us despite Brecht's intention. We are nevertheless able to understand his play in the way he wanted us to. The way we, the audience, inhabited the space, made the experience more than just a spectacle being played out before us, as if on a screen. And importantly it wasn't a case of cinema doing it better. Frankly, circus films are awful. They don't work because they entirely miss the point, which is that you have to be there in the circus audience.

In a cinema show, the distance between you in the audience and the picture on the screen is empty. It's a dead gap. Its only function is to carry as much light as is needed to see the film. You are not a part of what's going on on the screen and no amount of illusory tricks can change this reality. In fact, they reinforce it. And isn't watching a film at home alone, on the TV screen, the same experience as watching the film in the cinema? The only difference is that the screen is smaller and any effects less spectacular. Isn't it nice to be on your own without all those other people? The audience in the cinema can be something of an irritation! This is an important point. It's not simply some abstract philosophical argument such as a piece of theatre cannot exist without an audience because no one is watching it – while a film can. In its can!

But while circus, like theatre, has live action and live audience, it doesn't have story. In the circus there is no identifiable emotional journey. You may make one up but it's not one the whole audience will share. Cinema has story but we know it's different from theatre in that the experience of the audience is different. Put at its most simple, to restate the point: a film doesn't need an audience and you don't need to be in an audience to experience it.

So how *is* theatre different? And what makes it unique amongst the arts? I think it ought to be like this: In Theatre you have an enclosed space filled with live people in the audience and live people on stage. The apparent gap between the audience and the action on stage is, unlike in the cinema, full and fraught. There is an inter-connectedness that makes what is going on in this space a *society*. In one sense, it's an alternative society. You may see it as a microcosm of society at large. It's a society separated from society at large only by its special purpose.

Societies live on stories. In order to understand themselves and to progress they analyse their stories. In society at large this is called *history*. In more specialist areas it's called *philosophy*, and elsewhere *the social sciences*. In that space where these people have congregated it's called *Theatre*. The people on the stage in Theatre have come out of the audience. Their roles are interchangeable. The reason they're all there is to analyse a story. The story is about a problem. In the complex of society at large it's not possible to see the problem clearly, so someone is hired who has special skills, to focus the problem and outline it clearly and prepare the analysis: the playwright.

In order to make it clearer and to make it a more democratic process, the writer borrows people from the audience to create a picture of his analysis that they can all engage in. We are all alive, present and of the same species – not as in a film where you are able to watch the acting of the dead! In Theatre the event is all-embracing. Ideally, the space would be filled with people from all the different classes in society and all walks of life. After all, what's happening here is something that concerns everyone. Remarkably, the endeavour is entertaining! But it's not entertaining in the way that the clown in the circus may be entertaining, in the sense that he simply makes you laugh as if he'd tickled you. It's entertaining because of the journey of discovery you've all gone on. It has a suspense, but it's not a suspense that's manipulated by some wicked master to cause you, say, to be shocked. It's a suspense that comes out of the revelations, out of the unravelling of the problem. Not a suspense like waiting for the girl to get to her trapeze, or perhaps failing, but one filled with the knowledge that one day she'll find what she's really looking for. In fact, the delight in this entertainment is derived from the authority you discover in the exercising of your intelligence in seeing, with the other people in the space, the working out of the problem. If you like, the difference between the entertainment offered in the circus ring and the entertainment experienced in Theatre is the difference between mere pleasure and real happiness. A society that pursued only pleasure and not happiness would, I think, be doomed to extinction. I think that goes for Theatre, particularly when one considers that cinema does it better.

As I've already suggested, I would say that for Theatre to work, for it to fulfil itself, the relationship, based on this analysis, between audience and stage is an active even a creative one, and, of course, a moral one. They're embarked on the same quest. But Contemporary British Theatre is Director's theatre and, I'm sorry to say, I think that many of our theatre directors behave like film directors.

I mentioned earlier how the only function of the otherwise dead space between the audience and the screen in cinema is to carry just enough light as is needed for you to see the film. That quantity of light is decided by the director and it's just enough to let you see *his* vision. What you see is, if you like, non-negotiable. It's essentially one person's vision. Of course there is a kind of collaborative process between the director and the designer, the cinematographer and the editor but, ultimately this collaboration serves the one vision: the director's. In no way is it like the collective experience of theatre. In the theatre, the collaboration is between the audience and the stage. There is no collaboration between the audience and what takes place on the screen. You may say: but the audience doesn't affect what takes place on the stage in the theatre. This is the important point. It's the audience *expectation* which affects the stage. And I don't mean a *particular* audience like, say, the audience that goes to The Barbican or the audience that goes to The Cottesloe; I mean the audience that *is* society. And that expectation is that the writers will write plays that open up the debate between audience and stage. Of course, there is going to be a conflict between the writer who understands his professional responsibility to theatre in this way and the director who wants to be a whiz kid and would really rather be making films.

There is another point: film essentially has a moral silence at its heart, because you the audience can't debate with it. Director led theatre which in effect mimics film also has a moral silence at its core. But acting in the theatre must be a moral activity! Actors have to connect morally with the morality of the play. How can actors act in a moral vacuum? They can't. So they don't understand stage acting and then can't act the plays the responsible playwright wants to write. But it's the playwright who's blamed for not writing a play they can act, while it's really the director's fault for not wanting to direct plays properly.

In theatre, the director's role ought to be simply to facilitate the audience's access to the play which will enable them to engage creatively with the debate. The director should *never*, as happens in cinema, bring to bear his or her vision and interpretation on what takes place in theatre and by so doing decide for the audience how to interpret what it sees. To me, this is anti-democratic. It thwarts theatre's purpose. It's no different, really, from dictatorship in society, but it happens. We've already seen how big, how important our directors are. They even get credited in a curious hybrid way with authorship of an important play! By showing off *their* creative talents they deprive the audience of its own creative role. Analytical theatre gets marginalised if not eased out altogether.

In his Commentary on the *War Plays* Edward Bond talks about this relationship between society and theatre. It's a similar argument put a little differently. He writes under the sub-title: **We are sent to the Theatre:**

In the early world of jungles and deserts, and in the classical world of fifth century Athens, the whole community went to the drama. If slaves, convicts, the mad and women were sometimes excluded, that is because they were not fully members of society. Society sends people to the drama just as it sent them to the fields, the hunt and the well. It seems that now we are not sent to the theatre but choose to go. This is an illusion. We are still sent there by society. It must send us to the theatre even when it can only send representatives. It needs theatre as much as it needs its other institutions – its prisons, universities, parliaments and so on. But just as democratic society wrongly assumes that everyone in it, and not merely the ruling class, has power, so when society sends representatives to the theatre, it is sending the community there. Unjust society not only manipulates force by disguising violence as law and order, it also manipulates the rest of culture. Just as it usually sends the wrong people to prison and parliament, so it usually sends the wrong people to the theatre. The other it sends to the petrified drama of most film and television – and their frenetic activity is a sign of their moribund state: giving electric shock to a skeleton does not bring it to life.

(Bond, 1985: 259)

Interesting about Bond: a contemporary British dramatist who many serious theatre thinkers and commentators throughout the world consider one of *the* great dramatists of the twentieth century has been practically frozen out of contemporary British Theatre. Interestingly for us his play *In The Company Of Men*, which we may include in our category of plays about the professions, has been playing to full houses in Paris while here its production at the Barbican in 1996 was received with malice. I think what Bond means, at least in part, is that the working class aren't sent to the theatre. If theatre is about – as I believe it is – debate (to put it at its most simple) then you can't have a debate with only one side in attendance. And in our society, the social debate is between the classes. I hope the connections I'm making are becoming clear. What seems clear enough to me is that if Contemporary British Theatre is as I've suggested, is really Director's theatre where analytical theatre is not wanted, then it's clear why it appeals in the main to the middle classes. Ironically, for me, perhaps, the professional classes. It's *because* they don't need to have their society analysed to understand their position in it. Theatre then has a different function. It's one in which, in the main, their complacency is shored up or at best their liberal views are given reassurance. But it's not Theatre. It's what I call theatrical events produced for a particular audience and not the universal audience Theatre looks for. It's when this kind of theatrical event predominates at the expense of Theatre, that you get the kind of grotesque discussion I saw a few weeks ago on *Newsnight* when, in discussing Labour's Welfare-to-Work philosophy, the 'drama' referred to as approximating some kind of commentary on this was not some play on at the Royal Court, say, but *The Full Monty* – a film!

Before I go on to talk about *Wittgenstein's Daughter*, I'd like to briefly restate my arguments. As a playwright I have come to see that Contemporary British Theatre is failing. If I may make a joke: it makes how theatre deals with any subject, including the professions, purely academic. It's failing because most of its audience is middle-class, and while its moral duty ought to be to monitor the other professions, which collectively shape our society, on behalf of the rest of society, it can't because a part of that society is excluded from the theatre in general terms all but irrelevant and produces a moral silence at its heart. I am a working-class writer and so have a duty to address the problem of this moral silence, if you like, on behalf of my class. The moral silence has caused those who work in the theatre to confuse it with, primarily, cinema, and has caused them to lose sight of theatre's *unique purpose*. My play *Wittgenstein's Daughter* is an attempt to understand this moral silence and to dramatise the arguments that surround it. It has been said to me: how can you call yourself a working class playwright when your plays – especially a play like *Wittgenstein's Daughter* – are so intellectual. I reply: What, you think the working class have no intelligence? In fact, the working class has a greater need for the use of intellect than anyone else! But it's denied the right to use it. The professions, by which I mean, in the main, the media though also our professional politicians and so on, have made the intellectual investigation of the working class in particular by the working-class, unfashionable. They even deny that the working class exists! In the main, I don't write about the working-class. Why is this? If the audiences in our theatres are predominantly middle-class, why write about the working class. The only purpose could be to paint a kind of sentimental picture which will amuse the middle-class or create a kind of horror story that will invoke pity. I don't think you can write a play analysing the conditions of the working class by writing a play about only the working class. This is because those conditions are instituted by the middle class and reinforced by its language. You can't discuss, if you like, the nature of oppression without analysing the language it's couched in, and that language would be absent from a play that's just about the working class. I'm afraid the kind of play you end up with is a play that's like the famous 1930s photograph of the family of dust-bowl refugees, taken during the American Depression when the farmland in Oklahoma turned to dust, and the Oakies, as they were called, migrated to California. A middle-class photographer Dorothea Lange came from New York to take some pictures. When she returned to New York she had in her possession a photograph of a mother and her children – called Migrant Mother – which had about it a rare quality. It seemed to capture in a very poetic way all the suffering of this dispossessed people. The liberals of New York threw dinner parties around reproductions of the photo and cried into their wine. It didn't really explain anything and it did nothing for the Oakies whom you would have thought belonged to an entirely different society. It was just that the whole terror of the calamity seemed caught in that pose and it allowed them their comforting cathartic weep – the kind of thing that Brecht so despised. Dorothea Lange, like one of our middle-class slice-of-life dramatists, became a celebrity famous for her humanity and her eye: that she could have seen this moment of meaning in the meaninglessness of the maelstrom. In fact, what she did was to exploit the terrible condition of these almost unbearably lost people – for it came out that the photo was a fake. The family's pose had been directed by the photographer. In the same way, the working class is exploited in plays about them in our middle-class theatre. It's what Germaine Greer recently called the pornography of representation.

Like it or not, it's not that the working class have no intelligence, but that, as I've already indicated, they have a repressed intelligence. It contributes to their particular silence. I'm not going to go into a history of industrial society or quote Marcuse to prove this. I don't need to. I grew up in this environment. It gets into the collective psyche. The proof of it can be found in the way that the sense of guilt created can produce a hatred for the intellectual among the working class. The tool of this oppression is *language*. The result is, as I've already suggested, *different* languages.

Although people appear to speak the same language, such as English, they are in fact speaking different languages. For example, and it's a simple example, the working class confronted with a problem – maybe some kind of prohibition – might say (collectively):

We can't do that.

whereas the middle class faced with exactly the same problem would be more likely to say collectively:

We must find a way of overcoming the problem so that we are able to do that.

I am, as a working-class writer, using the second language as a means of understanding the relationship between the two.

I wanted to write a play about the moral silence. To analyse it dramatically, to bring it to an audience and by being entertained by the way I tell the story, engage with it and perhaps come to an understanding of the problems. I knew of Wittgenstein's famous declaration invoking silence in matters moral, and though I didn't study Wittgenstein at University, nor am I a linguistic philosopher, I guessed it would be a good place to begin. After all Wittgenstein *was* a philosopher of language.

His early work the *Tractatus Logico Philosophicus*, as I've already mentioned, concludes with the famous line: 'whereof one cannot speak one must remain silent' – the 'whereof' referring to morality. Basically, it seemed to me, what Wittgenstein was saying in this work was that the only things we can talk about with certainty are tautologies: the propositions of scientific fact such as, say, *a triangle has three sides*. Three sides is contained in the idea of the triangle ???? Nothing else, including morality, can be spoken about with this certainty. What Wittgenstein means by silence is an absence of appropriate language. Which is why it's in the silence where everything that matters resides. This was a thrilling idea. It seemed that this is the way *I* was thinking about silence.

I came to reflect at this time on a lecture I'd attended while studying for a PGCE at Cambridge in 1980. The lecturer – a leading Cambridge educationalist – detailed a strategy for teaching in a Comprehensive School which was liberal and to my mind just a little cavalier. I was furious with what he had to say because I knew that his liberal ideas – basically the abandoning of teaching the grammar of language and the grammar of mathematics and so on – would encourage laziness in teachers and lead to the kids of my class being deprived of a detailed enabling kind of education, while those kids who would one day find themselves in Oxbridge Universities would have a very different kind of education in their private, so-called public schools – an education which would be all embracing and enabling. In the end the *language* of the working-class kid at Comprehensive School would be diluted, stripped of its need to question; its ability to analyse and any sense it may have of its own authority. It would be a subject language which would provide an increasingly unheard voice. Of course, it's happened. I felt deeply betrayed by these professionals and left Cambridge after a term. It seemed to me that here, in effect, were the seeds of a conspiracy – but one achieved, perhaps, or perhaps not, by default rather than something actively pursued.

Then I was introduced to a book written by an American, William Warren Bartley III, which contained a very dramatic argument. Put at its simplest, the argument was that Wittgenstein was a closet homosexual who conceived a moral philosophy, the terms of which would prevent any discussion of his sexuality!

Next, I came across Fukuyama's *end of history* idea. What Fukuyama seemed to be saying in the wake of the collapse of the Soviet Union was that in this now post-modern world, politics would everywhere find a centre ground, that there would be no opposition and we would find ourselves forever subject to an overwhelming, amorphous middle class. Fukuyama was a philosopher and here was this philosopher telling us that in post-modernism there would be no voice for anything *but* the middle class! An argument for a moral silence at the core! This was a refinement of my conspiracy theory!

I had become by this time, after eleven or twelve years of Thatcherism and Kinnock's collaboration, deeply concerned about what was happening to our societal values. In particular our socialist values. If *bourgeois* meant, in some sense, that value had become *extrinsic* i.e. measured by how much a thing was worth in monetary terms (especially a human being) rather than *intrinsic* – which is what I believed bourgeois to mean, then we were living in the apotheosis of bourgeois society of which Fukuyama's theory was a symptom rather than a proof. A symptom which describes the moral silence.

I felt that the story needed to be some kind of investigation which brought me to Wittgenstein's second major work, which appeared at the end of his life, *The Investigations. This* work of Wittgenstein was saying that language was actually a game within the boundaries of which we, its users, are trapped. We can never get outside. So we can never be objective and can never, therefore, speak the truth. We don't even have the tautologies of the *Tractatus*. But if the working class doesn't even have the possibility of access to a language which might tell the truth about their condition – even though they may have to struggle through minefields to get to it – what is there? What weapon can they have?

Another piece of what was clearly becoming a jigsaw puzzle then arrived. In some ways it was the most devastating piece for me in my dealings with the betrayals of the professions. It concerned the philosopher, Paul de Man, who, I discovered, had used the new philosophy of de-constructionism, which seemed to incorporate Wittgenstein's language of non-truth, in order to rewrite his own history and hide from the world his own crimes as a fascist in the Second World War.

Then I was sent a cutting from a newspaper. I believe it was *The Independent.* It was by Danah Zohar and was about de-constructionism and its associate philosophy, referring to Fukuyama, Wittgenstein, post-Modernism, and Derrida – which was of great interest to me.

What it looked like was this: Wittgenstein's philosophy, which, to put it crudely, contended that you cannot use language to tell the truth, was used by Paul de Man (and perhaps others) to duck responsibility for his crimes against society. And maybe it would be used ultimately to deny the holocaust! And also, according to Bartley's book, Wittgenstein's whole argument was derived from his desire to surround his homosexuality with silence. So I needed to bring these things together by means of some kind of investigation. Then I could, in dramatic form, analyse my own arguments around the question of the professional's responsibility to society, in particular the subject classes and how those classes remain subject through the manipulation of language.

Of course, such a drama will be a kind of language game itself, but for me it is acceptable if, in pursuit of its serious intention, the play is playful.

The final piece of what I needed to make my play came when Robert David Macdonald, the director at the Citizen's Theatre in Glasgow, suggested to me that the play needed a woman. Suddenly everything became clear. If Wittgenstein was a homosexual the chances are he wouldn't have a daughter – which he didn't; and if the philosophy had originated in this need to obscure the facts of his homosexuality then couldn't the creation of a daughter also have this effect. And if there is a woman known as Wittgenstein's daughter then wouldn't it be reasonable to construct a play around her need to discover, precisely, her identity? A search like the young woman's search for the trapeze. An investigation!

Now I needed a starting point. Zohar's newspaper article had begun:

'In *Alice's Adventures in Wonderland*, the Dodo introduces Alice to the notion of a Caucus-race. He marks out some space with no particular shape, various creatures stand around in it 'here and there', and in quite random fashion some of them run about. 'There was no 'one, two, three and away', but they began when they liked, and left off when they liked, so it was not easy to know when the race was over.' It is an irrational way to run a race, a race with no centre, no rules, no authority and no purpose ...'

(Zohar)

This seemed a reasonable place to begin. This is talking about language stripped of meaning. My Alma, the name I had given to my heroine, would be a kind of Alice only her journey would not be quite so benign. As I say in the notes to the play:

'Post Modernism with its uncertainty is like a mine-field ... . Alma struggles through this minefield in which philosophical truth is caricatured as lie *or* in which simple lie masquerades as philosophical truth. Her journey is through a post-holocaust, Post Modern landscape in which history seems to mean nothing and values are manipulated by the dead as, perhaps, in a nightmare.'

(Edwards, 1993: 7)

The way I would do it would be this way: Alma at the beginning is without language – in the way that I've described. But she knows things aren't right. In a sense, as soon as the play begins, I would have her begin her journey of coming into language. I decided that she should be pregnant then she would have someone she would want to give a language to. Everything seems to her without meaning. I would have to show this. Maybe she lives with a husband she doesn't admire because he is somehow a purveyor of anti-meaning. I would have her driven by this emptiness to go in search of her own history – which would mean finding the traces, as it were, of her father. She must go to Cambridge, but there she should discover that there's been a conspiracy to deny her her real history and consequently her language. She should unravel the conspiracy, and in so doing empower herself and give herself a language – the meaningful language which she can then give to her child.

The play opens with Alma in Paris. She has come there with her husband Celine who is a member of the French National Front and is to make a speech at their conference. His speech is to be on the end of history. She is despondent. To begin with, she has no language of her own. She complains about her husband, about how

'he brings home terrible phrases …' by which she means clichés, 'like other men bring
  home friends …'

and yet she herself speaks in cliché:

'I am overwhelmed by clichés to the point where I can do nothing about it: trapped
  between the devil and the deep blue sea.'

She argues with him half-heartedly. He is already denying the holocaust. He dresses and leaves. A concierge arrives with a television. They talk. He's working-class. English. So is she, of course. She thinks he's coming onto her sexually. He tells her he's gay. This causes her to feel at ease and she's able to confide in him. But it's as if he is a nobody, as if he doesn't really exist. A cypher. This is why she can speak to him about these things which are otherwise cloaked in silence. She tells him that she's pregnant, and that her husband doesn't know. She tells him of her worries about bringing a child into this world. At the end of history! It comes out that her father was Wittgenstein. He tells her that she shouldn't bring a child into a world that she perceives has no values. She tells him about a Mr Beckett , who lives in Cambridge, who knew her father, and the Concierge tells her that she should leave her husband and look this Beckett up. He says:

CON: … Your old man [meaning Wittgenstein] must have had a few ideas which maybe
       he imparted to this Mr Beckett who you may now speak to as though *he* were your
       father. This will help you decide whether to have your baby or not. I would say
       you can't go wrong with a dead, revered philosopher as your father. You'll be in
       any aura he left behind. I'd say you were onto a winner.

Alma leaves her husband and goes to Cambridge where she looks up Beckett, who is an ex-boxer and now one-hundred-and-one years old. He reluctantly lets her in but is not pleased to see her. She has brought him a present of a book (the Bartley book with the argument about Wittgenstein's homosexuality). He tells her that his television doesn't work and asks her to go and get someone to look at it. She says there must be a Currys in town and goes. He asks her not to come back. As soon as she's gone, Wittgenstein's Ghost turns up.

The Ghost tells Beckett that he (Beckett) has to accept the woman as Wittgenstein's Daughter even though it, the Ghost, doesn't know where she's come from. Alma returns. The Ghost is put into a closet. Alma hasn't been to the television shop. There are things she wants to clear up with Beckett. Beckett shows her photographs of Wittgenstein and her mother. Beckett tells her that Carrington, an old student of Wittgenstein, is coming to dinner but there is no food; would she go out again and buy some fish and chips. She goes and the Ghost returns. The Ghost is to become Carrington. Beckett bandages the Ghost's head having told Alma that the old man has had his face eaten away by cancer. While Beckett bandages the Ghost's head he lies to the Ghost telling it how the plot to get Wittgenstein a child was carried out by a group of his students. We discover that Beckett was Wittgenstein's first lover.

During the meal, the book Alma has brought – the Bartley book – is discussed. Things get heated and the Ghost becomes angry, stuffing Alma's mouth full of chips when the truth about Wittgenstein's homosexuality is revealed. Not only that but Beckett's lie about the group of student's is discovered. Beckett is the man who impregnated her mother and Alma knows now that he is, therefore, her father.

Alma falls asleep. When she wakes, Beckett has gone leaving a note behind saying that he's gone to St Giles's Cemetery. Alma feels certain that this must be where her mother is buried. As she is about to leave she finds in a newspaper that was used to wrap up the chips, the Zohar article. She reads it with its argument that Wittgenstein had killed philosophy just as Nietzsche had killed God. She reads of, I quote:

> '… contemporary thinkers who have made it their declared aim to undo philosophy, to chip away at the foundations of thought and of the self who thinks, to shock and undermine – to de-construct – the beholder's sense of reality … the end of philosophy thinkers claim there is no deep truth waiting to be discovered. In place of truth or reality, we have only limited human discourse … .'

She reads about Paul de Man and concludes that Wittgenstein is responsible for her own *angst*, not to mention, in a curious way, her own husband's fascism. The article brings things together for her (as it had done for me, the writer) and gives her, through the understanding it offers, that authority which is the basis of the ownership of language.

Young Beckett – who is also the ghost of Beckett, and the Concierge at the beginning – has appeared with Beckett at Wittgenstein's grave (not Alma's mother's) and tells the old man to dig up the body and lay the skeleton out as a statement of pure language. Beckett does this and dies collapsing onto the skeleton as though he were making love to it. Alma arrives and believes that the skeleton must be her mother. She removes the dead Beckett and herself lays on the skeleton, fondling the bones tenderly and speaks to them about her pregnancy and her worries and then, about her new determination that's come with her being able to speak about these things. Then she sees the headstone and discovers that it's actually Wittgenstein's grave. Angrily, she puts her hand inside Wittgenstein's skull as though looking for the traces of the mind that has so influenced her life. Finding nothing there she gives birth at the grave of Wittgenstein while hitting out with two of Wittgenstein's bones to fight off the pain.

The play is straightforward: Alma's husband – the fascist, wants to talk about *the end of history* – a distinctly fascist notion. Alma goes in search of her identity prompted by the Concierge, a cypher who represents her working-class origins – being an incarnation of her father, Beckett. He spurs her on to overcome his own sense of guilt (the working class are often the footsoldiers of the fascists) at his own part in the collaboration between the classes which would deprive the working class of its language. She walks into a conspiracy which seeks to silence her and deny her her history by maintaining the idea that she is Wittgenstein's Daughter, carrying the book about Wittgenstein that, for my dramatic purpose at least, tells the truth that Wittgenstein has sought to cover up. Alma is finally able to speak – to possess a language which is the expression of her own authority – with the aid of the Zohar article that explains so much for her. She has created a language and a moral presence for herself by applying her intellect to the deepest philosophical arguments that arise from her case. She has brought light out of darkness. Language out of silence.

In the notes to the play I have written:

> 'There is a conflict between the real language of being human and the apparent language of everyday discourse. To a large extent it's that conflict upon which my dramatic intention writhes. The outcome, I hope, is an expression of the human condition and even a search for the meaning of that.'

We might say that apparent language is the language of the professional classes while real language is the language of the humanity tortured by the language of the professional classes. In a sense, this language is an ideal language – the language of real democracy – the language the housepainter would have liked to have had in his dealings with the vet. In the following note I write:

> For most of the play, the real language of being human is one Alma can't use. Because what she might want to talk about – the birth of her baby, she can't speak of. Not until she's gone through the minefield. The play goes from the cliché to *the world*, i.e. the synthesis achieved between Alma's quest [for real language] and the history of Beckett and the Ghost related through an apparent language [the language of biography]. The dramatic synthesis is achieved at the moment of Alma being able to speak about her child-to-be (at Wittgenstein's grave). The play is utterly simple but fraught.

At the very beginning she is not able to speak about her own pregnancy. The only person she can tell is the Concierge who, in a sense, doesn't even exist. The words she speaks are powerless. Awash in the flood of time, what spurs her on is the moral drive of noumenal history. It sets her off on her quest. The play is playful. It knows none of the boundaries Wittgenstein may have imposed on language. It doesn't pander to realism. As I've said, cinema does this better. It attempts to look inside the skull, into the noumenal realities. The only rules it may acknowledge are those of Drama. When we think of the Concierge as the Young Beckett, for example, then we have the irony of Beckett setting her on the trail that will reveal what he did. But, of course, because it cannot be the Young Beckett, the irony becomes something more subtle: a paradox.

And this is the central paradox for humanity: that in the lie resides the truth. And in the silence, real language.

The *end of history* is a phrase. It's also the sub-title of the play: Scenes at the end of history. At the beginning, Alma's fascist husband Celine is going to use it in his speech to the National Front Conference. He is going to argue that there is no more Communism – or Socialism for that matter – and that the stage is set for the fascist millennium. This will come about because there is no more opposition. It will come out of the middle class which will grow and grow. Wittgenstein's Ghost argues against history by denying Alma hers – it's something to be manipulated, as Paul de Man manipulated it, to hide the truth. But the end of history is a paradox. The mere statement of the idea proves that history lives. The phrase causes us to wonder at how language can be used to make this claim despite ourselves. We are history. We are history in the making.

The end of history of the sub-title not only refers to Fukuyama's theory but to Alma's condition. Until she finds out the truth she has no history. That history which is a working-class one. Nor does she have a language. There is only the moral silence. As I suggested at the beginning, her struggle to discover that history, her language, whatever, is also the struggle of the play. She has been denied that history by the professionals and the collusion of her father Beckett and even that of her sad mother, whose condition, one might say, is the quintessential condition of the working class: the whore. Or is this the oldest profession?

At one point in the late eighties, before the Citizens Theatre in Glasgow made its commitment to the play, the Royal Court were interested in my Wittgenstein idea. Or I should say, the courageous Michael Hastings who was, at the time, literary manager. He managed to get me some money from a fund they had. I'd considered having two Wittgenstein's: the dying one and his ghost and the ghost would be responsible for bringing the past to life and deal with the Bartley allegations. Michael felt he couldn't push this idea: one Wittgenstein was quite enough for these people – which included the Artistic Director – who had thought, anyway, that Wittgenstein was a pack of cigars! Michael eventually had to abandon me and my idea in the face of this ignorance.

I've tried to show that I believe that the way that theatre should deal with the professions is to recognise that they have a particular responsibility to the society they authorise, as it were; that theatre itself has a deeper responsibility as the profession that *keeps an eye* on those other professions which order our society. The monitor of democracy. That purpose is not just a moral and aesthetic one but one that it makes theatre relevant. My worry is that instead of being society in microcosm charged with the business of analysing society at large by the application of the dramatic aesthetic to a particular problem, it's actually becoming (or behaves as) an often dirty little pursuit for the gratification only of those in attendance. An environment heady with the air of complacency. Places where there is an overwhelming sense of self-congratulation lost on most people outside its confining walls. And usually that congratulation is directed at the Director – for we have Director's theatre.

The play *Wittgenstein's Daughter* is very much about my own struggle with and within Theatre. I said at the beginning that I can't separate the making of the play from what the play is about. The conspiracy at the heart of the play is a mirror image of the conspiracy to silence my kind of theatre. The birth at the end of the play is the birth of my work over the grave of radical, political, analytical theatre.

Bibliography

Ackroyd, P., *T. S. Eliot*, London, Hamilton, 1984.

Althusser, L., 'Ideology and Ideological State Apparatuses', in *Lenin and Philosophy*, trans. Ben Brewster (London, NLB, 1971), pp. 121–73.

Andrews, E., *The Art of Brian Friel: Neither Reality Nor Dreams*, London, Macmillan; New York, St. Martin's Press, 1995.

Anonymous, *Passion Killers* Programme, Hull Truck Programme for first tour of *Passion Killers* after premieres at Hull and Derby, 1995.

Anonymous, 'The Long Journey Home', *The Independent*, 22 June 1994, p. 23.

Anonymous, 'World Without End', *The Sunday Times*, 26 September 1976, p. 35.

Anthony, A. *et al*, 'Acts in a Sex War', *The Guardian, G2*, 7 July 1993, p. 2.

Aston, E. and Savona, G., *Theatre as Sign-System: a Semiotics of Text and Performance*, London and New York, Routledge, 1991.

Ayckbourn, A., *Season's Greetings*, London, French, 1982.

Barber, J., *Daily Telegraph*, 10.2.1984.

Barrett, J., *Borrowed Robes*, Dublin, 1998. (unpublished typescript)

Barrett, J., 'Dogs, Ducks, and Dissent – A 'Priest Play' on Tour in Ireland', in Kurdi, M., Hartvig, G. and Rouse, A. C. (eds.) *Focus: Papers in English Literary and Cultural Studies* (Pécs, University Press Pécs, 2000), forthcoming.

Barthes, R., *Mythologies* [1957] trans. Annette Lavers, London, Paladin, 1973.

Benjamin, W., *One Way Street and Other Writings*, trans. by E. Jephcott and K. Shorter, Norfolk, Verso, 1985.

Bennett, A., *The Madness of George III*, London, Faber, 1992.

Bennett, J., Unpublished interview with John Godber, June 30, 1997.

Berger, D. A., 'Künstlerdethronisierung als dramatisches Prinzip. Zur Ästhetik des Gegenwartstheaters in Großbritannien', in Thomsen, C.W. (ed.) *Studien zur Ästhetik des Gegenwartstheaters* (Heidelberg, Winter, 1985), pp. 209–224.

Berson, M., 'Whites Only in Fugard's *The Road to Mecca*', *San Francisco Chronicle Datebook*, 7 February 1988, p. 35.

Bertha, C., ''That Other world': the Mythic and the Fantastic in Contemporary Irish Drama' in Strewart, B. (ed.) *That Other World: Supernatural and the Fantastic in Irish Literature and its Contexts* (Gerard Cross, Colin Smythe, 1998).

Bhabha, H. K., *The Location of Culture*, London, Routledge, 1994.

Bhabha, H. K., 'Introduction: Narrating the Nation' in Bhabha, H. K. (ed.) *Nation and Narration* (London, Routledge, 1990), pp. 1–7.

Billington, M., *Bloody Poetry, The Guardian*, 2.11.1984.

Blass, M., 'Posting' Live Art mailing list, 1997.
    URL http: //www.mailbase.ac.uk/lists/liveart/archive.html

Bond, E., *War Plays*. London, Methuen, 1985.

Brenton, H., *Bloody Poetry*, London, Methuen, 1985.

Brilliant, R., *Portraiture*, London, Reaktion Books, 1991.

Broich, U. and Pfister, M. (eds.), *Intertextualität: Formen, Funktionen, anglistische Fallbeispiele*, Tübingen, Günter Narr, 1985.

Brown, S., 'Feminist Research in Archaeology' in Rabinowitz, N.S., and Richlin, A. (eds.) *Feminist Theory and the Classics* (New York and London, Routledge, 1993), pp. 238–71.

Brown, T., *Ireland: A Social and Cultural History 1922–85*, London, Fontana Press, 1990.

Buckley, T., 'Write me, said the Play to Peter Shaffer', *New York Times Magazine*, 13 April. 1975, pp. 20–40.

Capra, F., *The Turning Point: Science, Society and the Rising Culture*, London, Fontana, 1983.

Chaplin, S., letter to Stephen Di Benedetto, 3 September 1996.

Churchill, C. *Top Girls*, London, Methuen, 1991.

Clark, B., *Whose Life is it Anyway?*, London: French, 1978.

Clark, B., *The Petition*, Oxford, Amber Lane Press, 1986.

Cohn, R., 'Artists in Play' in Hutchings, W. (ed.) *David Storey: A Casebook* (New York / London, Garland Publishing, 1992), pp. 73–87.

Colvin, C., *Plays and Players*, April 1986, p. 21.

Cromwell, B., 'Peter Shaffer. The Two Sides of Theatre's Agonised Perfectionist', *The Times*, 28 April 1980.

Curtis, N., 'Technique: Time to Face Up to the Facts', *The Independent*, 26 January 1994.

Dantanus, U., *Brian Friel: A Study*, London, Faber and Faber, 1988.

de Olivera, N., Oxley, N., and Petry, M., *Installation Art*, London, Thames and Hudson, 1996.

Dewdney, A. K., 'Apfelmännchen', *Spektrum der Wissenschaft Sonderheft Computerkurzweil*, 1987, pp. 4–10.

Di Benedetto, S., unpublished interview with Stephen Bent, 12 March 1996.

Di Benedetto, S., Peter Snow in a private telephone conversation May 1996.

Dietrich, M., *Das Moderne Drama*, Stuttgart, 1974.

Edgar, D., *Mary Barnes*, London, Methuen, 1979.

Edwards, D., *Wittgenstein's Daughter*, London, Oberon, 1993.

Enkemann, J., 'Politisches Alternativtheater in Großbritannien', *EASt* 2 (1980).

Evans, M., 'Letter to the Editor', *The Times Literary Supplement*, 16.3.1984, p. 275.

Ferguson, M., *The Aquarian Conspiracy: Personal and Social Transformation in the 1980s*, London, Routledge and Kegan Paul, 1981.

Foster, R., *Modern Ireland 1600–1972*, London, Penguin Books, 1989.

Foucault, M., 'Nietzsche, Genealogy, History' in Rabonow, P. (ed.), *The Foucault Reader: An Introduction to Foucault's Thought* (London, Penguin, 1991), pp. 76–100.

Foucault, M., 'What is an Author?' in Rabonow, P. (ed.), *The Foucault Reader: An Introduction to Foucault's Thought* (London, Penguin, 1991), pp. 101–20.

Foucault, M., *The History of Sexuality: Volume 1*, trans. R. Hurley, Harmondsworth, Penguin, 1978.

Friel, B., *Selected Plays*, Washington D. C., The Catholic University of America Press, 1984.

Friel, B., *Making History*, London, Faber and Faber, 1989.

Friel, B., *Translations,* London, Faber and Faber, 1981.

Furse, A., *Augustine (Big Hysteria)*, Amsterdam, Harwood Academic, 1997.

Gadamer, H-G., *Truth and Method*, trans. J. Weinsheimer and D. G. Marshall, London, Sheed and Ward, 1989.

Garner, S. B., Jr., *Bodied Spaces: Phenomenology and Performance in Contemporary Drama*, Ithaca, Cornell University Press, 1994.

Gems, P., *Piaf*, Oxford, Amber Lane Press, 1979.

Glaap, A.-R., 'Gespräch mit Tom über Kempinski', Programme Notes to *Duet for One*, Düsseldorf, Kammerspiele, 1985.

Godber, J., *Aspects of the Dramatic Work of John Arden and David Storey*, unpublished M.A. thesis, School of English at the University of Leeds, May 1979.

Godber, J., interviewed by Sheena MacDonald for Radio 4's *Pebble in the Pond* series, 13 September 1997.

Godber, J., *Happy Families*, London, Samuel French, 1992.

Godber, J., *The Office Party*, London, Warner Chappell, 1995.

Godber, J., *Lucky Sods* and *Passion Killers*, London, Methuen, 1995.

Godber J., interviewed by Paul Allen for Radio 4's *Kaleidoscope*, 7 August 1997.

Goold, G.P. (ed.), *Sophocles' Fragments: The Searchers* trans. by Hugh Lloyd-Jones, LCL 483, Cambridge, Mass, Harvard University Press, 1996, pp. 140–177.

Gray, S., *Quartermain's Terms*, London, Methuen, 1983.

Gross, R., *Understanding Playscripts: Theory and Method*, Bowling Green, OH, Bowling Green University Press, 1974.

Hagelin, J., 'Is Consciousness the Unified Field? A Field Theorist's Perspective', *Modern Science and Vedic Science*, 1 (1987), pp. 29–88.

Hallam, J., 'Unequal Opportunities? Gender and Professionalism in the Medical Melodrama', unpublished paper, 1997.

Hampton, C., *Tales From Hollywood*, London, Faber and Faber, 1983.

Hare, D., *Racing Demon*, London, Faber and Faber, 1990.

Hare, D., *Asking Around*, London, Faber and Faber, 1993.

Harrison, T., *The Common Chorus: A Version of Aristophanes' Lysistrata*, London and Boston, Faber and Faber, 1992.

Harwood, R., *The Dresser*, Oxford, Amber Lane Press, 1980.

Hayman, R., *Playback*, London, Davis Poynter, 1973.

Hayman, R., *British Theatre Since 1955*: *A Reassessment*, Oxford, Oxford University Press, 1979.

Heijl, P. M., *Sozialwissenschaft als Theorie selbstreferentieller Systeme*, Frankfurt/Main, Peter Lang, 1982.

Herrnstein Smith, B., *Contingencies of Value: Alternative Perspectives for Critical Theory*, Cambridge/Massachusetts, Harvard University Press, 1988.

Hinsley C.M., 'Revising and Revisioning the History of Archaeology: Reflections on Region and Context' in Christenson, A. (ed.) *Tracing Archaeology's Past: The Historiography of Archaeology* (Carbondale and Edwardsville, Southern Illinois University Press, 1989), pp. 79–96.

Hoggart, R., *The Uses of Literacy*, Harmonsworth, Penguin, 1958.

Holt, J., *How Children Fail*, 2nd edn, Harmondsworth, Penguin, 1969.

Homden, C., *The Plays of David Hare*, Cambridge, Cambridge University Press, 1995.

Hughes, D., *Futurists*, London, Faber and Faber, 1986.

Hutchings, W. (ed.), *David Storey: A Casebook*, New York/ London, Garland Publishing, 1992.

Illich, I., *Deschooling Society*, 2nd edn, Harmondsworth, Penguin, 1973

Jordan, E., *The Feast of Famine: The Plays of Frank McGuinness*, Bern, Peter Lang, 1997.

Karpf, A., *Doctoring the Media: the Reporting of Health and Medicine*, London, Routledge, 1988.

Kavanagh, P., 'Father Mat' in Crotty, P. (ed.) *Modern Irish Poetry: an Anthology* (Belfast, The Blackstaff Press, 1995), pp. 42–46.

Kempinski, T., *Duet for One*, London, Samuel French, 1981.

Keogh, D., *Jews in Twentieth-Century Ireland: Refugees, Anti-Semitism and the Holocaust*, Cork, Cork University Press, 1998.

King, R. L., 'Language and Values in Hare's Plays' in Zeifman, H. (ed.) *David Hare: A Casebook* (New York and London, Garland Publishing, 1992), pp. 79–87.

Klaus, C.H., with Gilbert M. and. Field, B. S., Jr., (eds.) *Stages of Drama: Classical to Contemporary Theatre*, 3rd edn, New York, St. Martin's, 1995.

Kollbrunner, J., *Das Buch der Humanistischen Psychologie: Eine ausführliche einführende Darstellung und Kritik des Fühlens, Denkens und Handelns in der Humanistischen Psychologie*, Eschborn, Fachbuchhandlung für Psychiatrie, 1987.

Lacey, S., *British Realist Theatre: The New Wave in its Contexts, 1956–65*, London, Routledge, 1995.

Macaulay, A., 'A Playwright Scores Sweetly', *Financial Times*, 11 March 1995.

Macdonald, Keith M., *The Sociology of the Professions*. London: Sage, 1995.

McDonagh, M., *The Beauty Queen of Leenane*, London, Methuen, 1996.

McDonagh, M., *The Lonesome West*, London, Methuen, 1997.

MacDonald, S., *Not About Heroes*: *The Friendship of Siegfried Sassoon and Wilfred Owen*, London, Faber and Faber, 1983.

MacDonald, S., unpublished letter to D. Meyer-Dinkgräfe, 27 March 1985.

McDonough, Carla J., 'Every Fear Hides a Wish: Unstable Masculinity in Mamet's Drama' *Theatre Journal*, 44 (1992), pp. 195–205.

McGrath, F. C., *Brian Friel's (Post)Colonial Drama: Language, Illusion and Politics*, Syracuse NY, Syracuse University Press, 1999.

McGuinness, F., *Mary and Lizzie*, London, Faber and Faber, 1989.

Mamet, D., 'A candid conversation with America's foremost Dramatist about Tough Talk, TV Violence, Women, and Why Government Shouldn't Fund the Arts: interview by Geoffrey Norman and John Rezek', *Playboy*, 42: 2 (1995), pp. 52–3.

Mamet, D., *Oleanna*, London, Methuen, 1993.

Mamet, D., *Some Freaks*, New York, Viking, 1989.

Maturana, H., *Autopoiesis and Cognition: The Realisation of the Living*, Dordrecht, D. Reidel, 1980.

Merrimen, V., 'Decolonisation Postponed: The Theatre of Tiger Trash', *Irish University Review*, 29: 2 (1999), pp. 305–17.

Meyer-Dinkgräfe, D., unpublished interview with David Pownall, 4 March 1985.

Meyer-Dinkgräfe, D., unpublished interview with Roland Rees, 21 March 1985.

Meyer-Dinkgräfe, D., unpublished interview with Margaret Wolfit, 26 March 1985

Meyer-Dinkgräfe, D., unpublished interview with Howard Davies, 29 March 1985.

Meyer-Dinkgräfe, D., unpublished interview with Tom Wilkinson, 29 March 1985.

Munslow, A., 'The Plot Thickens', *The Times Higher Education Supplement*, 21 March 1997, p. 18.

Murray, C., *Twentieth-century Irish Drama: Mirror up to Nation*, Manchester, Manchester University Press, 1997.

Murray, C., 'Introduction' in Murray, C. (ed.) *Brian Friel: Essays, Diaries, Interviews: 1964–1999* (London, Faber and Faber, 1999), pp. VII–XXII.

Nichols, P., *The National Health: or, Nurse Norton's Affair*, London, Faber, 1970.

Nietzsche, F., 'On the Uses and Disadvantages of History for Life' in *Untimely Meditations* trans. by R. J. Hollingdale, Cambridge, Cambridge University Press, 1994, pp. 59–123.

Orton, J., *The Orton Diaries*, ed. John Lahr, London, Methuen, 1998.

Orton, J., *What the Butler Saw* in *Orton: The Complete Plays*, London, Methuen Drama, 1976.

O'Brien, E., *Virginia*, London, The Hogarth Press, 1981.

O'Connor, K., 'Audience put on the rack', *Sunday Times*, 9 Aug., 1998, p. 22.

O'Toole, F., *The Lie of the Land: Irish Identities*, London, Verso, 1997.

Pfister, M., *The Theory and Analysis of Drama*, Cambridge, Cambridge University Press, 1977.

Plato, *The Republic* trans: Desmond Lee, Penguin, London 1987.

Pownall, D., *Master Class*, London, Faber and Faber, 1983.

Price, M., *The Yale Review*, Summer, 1974, p. 517.

Prigogine, I. and Stengers, I., *Order Out of Chaos: Man's New Dialogue with Nature*, London, Heinemann, 1984.

Quigley, A., 'The Emblematic Structure and Setting of David Storey's Plays', *Modern Drama* 22 (1979), 259–76.

Ravenhill, M., *Shopping and F***ing*, London, Methuen, 1996.

Ravenhill, M., *Some Explicit Polaroids*, London, Methuen, 1999.

Rebellato, D., *1956 and All That: The Making of Modern British Drama*, London, Routledge, 1999.

Roberts, P. (ed.), *The Best of Plays and Players, Volume Two*, London, Methuen Drama, 1989.

Rusch, G., *Erkenntnis, Wissenschaft, Geschichte. Von einem konstruktivistischen Standpunkt*, Frankfurt/Main, Suhrkamp, 1987.

Rusinko, S., 'A Portrait of the Artist as Character in the Plays of David Storey' in Hutchings, William (ed.) *David Storey: A Casebook*, New York, Garland, 1992, 89–104.

Russell, W., *Educating Rita, Stags and Hens and Blood Brothers: Two Plays and a Musical*, London, Methuen, 1986.

Rutherford, M., 'Package Holiday Passions', *Financial Times*, 16 April 1994.

Said, E., *Culture and Imperialism*, London, Chatto and Windus, 1993.

Santner E. L., 'History Beyond the Pleasure Principle: Some Thoughts on the Representation of Trauma' in Friedlander, S. (ed.) *Probing the Limits of Representation: Nazism and the 'Final Solution'* (Cambridge, Mass, Harvard University Press, 1992), pp. 142–63.

Schmidt, J., *Grundriß einer empirischen Literaturwissenschaft*, Braunschweig und Wiesbaden, Vieweg, 1980.

Schorsch, C., *Die New Age Bewegung. Utopie und Mythos der Neuen Zeit. Eine kritische Auseinandersetzung*, Gütersloh, Bertelsmann, 1988.

Shaffer, P., *Equus*, London, Longman, 1993.

Shaffer, P., *Amadeus*, Burnt Mill, Longman, 1984.

Smith, A.C.H., 'Athol Fugard', Programme Notes, *The Road to Mecca*, National Theatre, London, 1985.

Sternlicht, S., 'Introduction' in Fitz-Simon, S. and Sternlicht, S. (eds.) *New Plays from the Abbey Theatre 1993–1995* (Syracuse, Syracuse University Press, 1996), pp. IX–XXIV.

Stinson, J., 'Dualism and Paradox in the 'Puritan' Plays of David Storey', *Modern Drama*, 20 (1977), pp. 131–143.

Storey, D., *Storey: Plays Three*, London, Methuen, 1998.

Storey, D., *Life Class*, in *Storey*, Harmondsworth, Penguin, 1980.

Storey, D., *Pasmore*, Harmondsworth, Penguin, 1976.

Storey, D., *Radcliffe*, Harmondsworth, Penguin, 1965.

Storey, D., 'Journey Through a Tunnel', in *The Listener*, 1 August 1963, pp. 159–61.

Taylor, C. P., *Good*, London, Methuen, 1982.

Taylor, J. R., *Anger and After: A Guide to the New British Drama*, London, Methuen, 1962.

Thompson, G., *Aeschylus and Athens*, London, Lawrence and Wishart, 1980.

Thornber, R., 'The Office Party', *The Guardian*, 8 September 1992.

Thornber, R., 'Passion Killers', *The Guardian*, 18 April 1994.

Todorov, T., *The Fantastic: A Structural Approach to a Literary Genre* trans. by Richard Howard, Ithaca, Cornell University Press, 1980.

Turow, J., *Playing Doctor: Television Storytelling and Medical Power*, New York, Oxford University Press, 1989.

Tynan, K., 'Review of *Look Back in Anger*', reprinted in Tynan, K. (ed.) *A View of the English Stage 1944–1965* (London, Methuen, 1984) pp. 176–9.

Tynan, K., *Tynan on Theatre*, Harmondsworth, Penguin, 1964.

Walker, Craig, 'Three Tutorial Plays: The Lesson, The Prince of Naples and Oleanna', *Modern Drama*, 40: 1 (1997), pp. 149–162.

Wardle, I., 'Wordy Verdi in the Stalls', *The Times*, 20 March 1986.

Wells, W., *Gertrude Stein and a Companion*, 1985.

Welsch, W., '*Postmoderne*: Genealogie und Bedeutung eines umstrittenen Begriffs', in Kemper, P. (ed.) *Postmoderne oder Der Kampf um die Zukunft. Die Kontroverse in Wissenschaft, Kunst und Gesellschaft* (Frankfurt/Main, Suhrkamp, 1988), pp. 9–36.

Westecker, D., 'Hatten sie wirklich Glück?', *Düsseldorfer Nachrichten*, 28.3.1983.

Wheatcroft, Geoffrey, 'Campus followers', *The Guardian* 16 September 1993 p. 22.

Bibliography

Wheeler, W., 'After Grief? What Kinds of Inhuman Selves?' in *New Formations: A Journal of Culture/Theory/Politics*, 25 (Summer 1995) *'Michel Foucault: J'accuse'*, pp. 77–95.

Williams, N., *A Little Like Paradise*, in Fitz-Simon, S. and Sternlicht, S. (eds.) *New Plays from the Abbey Theatre 1993–1995* (Syracuse, Syracuse University Press, 1996), pp. 247–315.

Wilson, A., "Our father': The Profession of Faith in *Racing Demon*' in Zeifman, H. (ed.) *David Hare: A Casebook* (New York and London, Garland Publishing, 1992), pp. 201–15.

Wing, B., 'The Office Party', *The Yorkshire Post*, 17 December 1992.

Wolfit, M., *George Eliot*. British Library, London, Playscript 807.

Wolter, J., 'Anger als dramtisierter Impuls. Gesellschaftskritik und gesellschaftliche Utopie seit 1945', in Kosok, H. (ed.) *Drama und Theater im England des 20.Jahrhunderts* (Düsseldorf, August Bagel, 1980).

Young, P., *Crystal Clear*, Harmondsworth, Penguin, 1983.

Zeifman, H., 'An Interview with David Hare' in Zeifman, H. (ed.) *David Hare: A Casebook* (New York and London, Garland Publishing, 1992), pp. 3–21.

Wesker, A., *Roots* in *The Wesker Trilogy*, Harmondsworth, Penguin, 1964.